Educating With Empathy

Educating With Empathy
A Holistic Framework for Teaching the Research Process

Dawn Rogers Stahura

Library Juice Press
Sacramento, CA

Copyright 2025

Published in 2025 by Library Juice Press.

Litwin Books
PO Box 188784
Sacramento, CA 95818

http://litwinbooks.com/

This book is printed on acid-free paper.

Publisher's Cataloging in Publication
Names: Stahura, Dawn Rogers.
Title: Educating with empathy : a holistic framework for teaching the research process / Dawn
     Rogers Stahura.
Description: Sacramento, CA : Library Juice Press, 2025. | Includes bibliographical references and
     index.
Identifiers: LCCN 2024950281 | ISBN 9781634001724 (acid-free paper)
Subjects: LCSH: Empathy – Study and teaching (Higher). | Research – Methodology – Study and
     teaching (Higher). | Instruction librarians – Professional relationships. | Academic librarians –
     Professional relationships.
Classification: LCC Z711.25.65 S73 2025 | DDC 028.7071--dc23
     LC record available at https://lccn.loc.gov/2024950281

Contents

1		**Foreword**
15	**Chapter 1**	**Spirit** Connection, Balance, Space
23	**Chapter 2**	**Educating with Empathy Framework**
27	**Chapter 3**	**Earth** Foundation, Building Blocks, Grounded
37	**Chapter 4**	**Act Up Evaluation Method**
45	**Chapter 5**	**Air** Vision, Strategy, Intellect
69	**Chapter 6**	**Water** Spirituality, Healing
85	**Chapter 7**	**Fire** Creation, Transformation
111		**Epilogue**
117		**Supplementary Material**
121		**Index**

*To H:
for meeting me at the crossroads
and showing me which path to take.*

*To my community at Salem State University,
this is for you.*

Foreword

I didn't always want to be a librarian. Growing up, I wanted to be a writer, an artist, a creator. I started my first journal when I was seven years old, documenting my life through my feelings and experiences. As I became more dependent on my journals, I completed two a year which required a few trips to the big mall an hour away so I could find blank journals at Waldenbooks. It took me forever to find the perfect journal. I would sit in front of the shelves of journals and carefully flip through their pages, imagining confiding my secrets into that blank interior. My mom always checked the price before agreeing to purchase them to which I replied, "One day when I am on Oprah, I am going to tell her how you scoffed at buying me $10.00 journals because you care more about the cost than my feelings." At fifteen years old, I imagined publishing my journals like Anais Nin (minus the sexiness). As I mowed the lawn I practiced my interview with Oprah, polishing my responses to her questions about my journal writing and the necessity of documenting one's interior life. I continuously tweaked the story I would tell of my mother and the purchasing of my journals. I imagined Oprah and I would laugh at the ridiculousness of my mom's price checking. Because obviously, creativity has no price tag. Later, I would learn what the absence of creativity truly cost me.

My father was an electrician with above-average artistic talent. His parents wanted him to go to art school where I believe he would have really honed his skills. Sadly, my father was a person who equated *real work* with getting your hands dirty. I envied his talent and wanted more than anything to draw like him. No matter how hard I tried, I just couldn't keep the connection between my mind and my hand. Sometime around 10 years old I decided I wasn't an artist and put away all my art supplies. I legitimately grieved my loss of artistic talent and longed for an existence where art and I were friends. During my senior year of high school, I took an art class just to fill up my schedule and rediscovered my love for art. The art teacher believed in positive reinforcement, and it almost convinced me I had actual talent until I took a few art courses part-time at a college two years later. To say that the professor was unkind is an understatement. While I understood the importance of grades, art is and always will be subjective. No matter how hard I worked I still received low marks and after one semester I dropped out and entered the workforce. All I was qualified to do was work as a grocery store clerk (did it), work the register at Dairy Queen (did it), and be a bank teller (did it). I grew up in a household where college was never talked about. Even if I had wanted to go to college straight out of high school, my parents couldn't afford it. I didn't really apply myself in my senior year of high school, so scholarships were out of the question. I took the SAT in my junior year only because my friend said we could check out the local record store afterwards. I'm pretty sure most of the points I received came from putting my name on the scantron sheet. No one in my immediate family had attended college so the whole idea that I would was inconceivable. By the time I turned 22 years old, I knew there had to be something else out in the world for me. I was tired and bored of working dead-end jobs in small-town Indiana and smoking pot to block out my depression and growing resentment toward all those who had 'made it out.'

As above so below

Art wasn't the only creative pursuit I had. At 14 years old, I thought I was a poet. I filled so many of those blank journals with rants and vignettes fueled by my anxiety and depression. I discovered poets like Sylvia Plath and Anne Sexton who had the ability to turn their despair into poems. Like so many young folx in the early nineties my depression went unchecked for decades. Writing was my form of therapy. I can admit to myself now that I should have been in therapy and medicated for what would become a high functioning anxiety disorder and bulimia. These two disorders plagued me for decades in ways I am still dealing with today. Sometime during my first year of high school, I discovered zines, and they literally saved my life. It was a form of writing I could do and the thought that I could publish it myself was a game changer. Publishing was now within my grasp as my father had a photocopier for his business. My early zines were very confessional and deeply personal. I wanted to be seen and heard even if I hid under a pseudonym. I made lifelong friends through zines. Friends I have had the pleasure of meeting in person after decades of being pen pals. Through zines, I discovered I was not alone. What I thought were isolated issues and situations happened quite frequently literally all over the United States. Within my zine pages, I got to own and speak my truth. Having a voice oftentimes comes with consequences and for me that arrived in the form of a suspension. During my senior year of high school, I was suspended for writing and distributing my zine on school grounds. I knew then that our stories matter. That our words matter. Despite being angry over the injustice of my punishment, I was fueled with the innate knowledge that our words have power, especially as a young woman, otherwise why would the institution attempt to silence me? This power couldn't be taken by the male-dominated school district then and it cannot be taken now by capitalism and toxic masculinity. The only things that have really changed are my age and location. Positionality matters.

In 1997 I enrolled at Purdue University in the Creative Writing program. The only way I managed to pay for school was by taking out a ridiculous amount of student alternative loans and working full-time. Throughout my four years of college, I was jaded and pissed off that I did not have the time to join clubs or attend events on campus because I was either doing homework or working. Even though leisure time felt nonexistent I kept reminding myself what the alternative was. I would die before I returned to rural Indiana. During my junior year, I decided to give myself one last chance and studied abroad in Florence at an art school hoping I could find my talent overseas. I felt so lost and out of place in artistic spaces and walked around Florence feeling like a fraud and epic failure. At the end of 1999, I once again packed up my art supplies and wouldn't think seriously of them again until I was in my 40s. It has taken me the greater part of my life to understand that talent does not equal creativity. That talent is not a requirement to create art and anyone who tells you otherwise is lying to you. I am done with the pretentious gatekeeping that keeps us from realizing our full potential as human beings. Creativity and the ability to create art is for everyone. EVERYONE. All that lost time away from art only fostered my deep connection to it and unconsciously led me down paths to incorporate creativity into not just my personal life but my librarian (professional) life as well. It has taken me a long time to call myself an artist. Hell, it has taken me years to call myself a writer and a poet. For some reason, these titles always felt like imposter syndrome when I attached them to my identity. But I am an artist. I am a writer. I am a poet. The things we are called to do will continue calling until we answer it. This I know now to be true.

I graduated in 2001 with a bachelor's degree in creative writing (poetry), a minor in Art and Design, substantial debt, and a burden of disillusionment in that you can't pay your bills with a poem. I was pissed off at the realization that a job was not the same thing as a career and I wanted the latter. After all that time and money, I was once again stuck at a dead-end job making minimum wage at the very institution that awarded my worthless degree. It was a rude awakening that I couldn't find a good-paying job with my degree. At least not in Indiana. My parents were proud that I graduated but were constantly reminding me that I had to repay my student loans as if I thought they would just go away on their own. I'll be honest. I toyed around with the idea of faking my own death but then I would remember that my dad was a co-signer so I would have to fake his death too and it all seemed suddenly too complicated. Too many deaths to contend with and I didn't have that kind of creative energy to pull it off. So, I busted my ass working my job to pay for the entry fees to poetry contests. I would submit poems weekly in the hopes of getting discovered. I did win two small poetry contests but in terms of fame? Not so much. My romantic notions of writing poetry while chain smoking and drinking wine were really just giving me sinus infections and a drinking problem. Who the hell wanted to read about that? Certainly not *The New Yorker*.

One night over margaritas with my best friend, Barbie, I said, "If I had to do it all over again, I would get my M.L.S. The only thing I really like about my job is the research I get to do for faculty." She looked at me and said, "You're not dead. Get your foot out of the grave and apply." Within the next month, I applied and was accepted as a full-time graduate student in the Library and Information Sciences program at Indiana University. I was hell bound to make this degree mean something no matter what it cost me. I graduated with my M.L.S. in 2009 while working a full-time job as a reference assistant at an academic library and a part-time job as a reference aide at the local public library clocking in around 62 hours a week. The way my work schedules played out, I was only off work four days a month. Utterly exhausted, I graduated with a 4.0 GPA, insomnia, a partial nervous breakdown, and a bad case of bulimia mixed with the occasional anorexia. I had my degree, but I felt like a husk of my former self. Indiana did not have the kind of job mobility I wanted or needed so I moved 1,000 miles away for my first professional librarian job where I knew absolutely no one. I moved away from a dead-end full-time job to a part-time job where money was so tight that I only had $125 left over a month after paying rent, utilities, student loan payments, and gas for my car. It was like being a broke college student all over again except this time I didn't have friends nearby to lean on. Despite the stress and anxiety of it all, I'm glad I had the courage to take that risk because it literally changed my entire life. I've had so many amazing opportunities in the way of teaching, instruction, research, presenting, mentoring, and zine-making. I've made some wonderful friends, colleagues, and accomplices. I've had incredible opportunities to try new things, develop and teach my own courses, create zine collections, and push against the status quo in surprising and awesome ways. I've watched students riddled with fear and then triumph in their final projects. I've listened to students share their stories through their zines and personal narrative writing that brought entire classrooms to tears. I've seen the way art can heal, empower, and build community. I've grown alongside students as an educator, learner, and human. Through my work, I have learned what empathy truly means and the impact it has inside and outside the classroom. I finally understand how the seemingly disparate pieces of my life actually come together in a cohesive and empathetic way, and it's nothing short of magical.

A 'medium' is literally a translator between realms of experience and/or realms of knowledge.

I am not *just* a librarian. I am a writer. I'm writing this book right now. I've written scholarly articles and academic presentations. I am a zinester. I've been creating zines since the 90s on one thing or another. I am a spiritual being, and this plays an integral role in everything I do but especially in my teaching and instruction, whether folx are aware of it or not. I am a feminist. I am queer. I am an artist. I am a poet. Here's the thing. I never needed any outside approval to embrace these facets and call them my own. I thought I did. In fact, we all think we do, and it is this fallacy that holds so many of us back from being our full, creative selves. Somewhere along the way, I embodied the false notion that talent equals creativity and that without talent you are not creative. You are not a writer or artist or dancer or whatever else you want to be because you don't have the 'talent' or the status or the paycheck or the devoted time that our dominant culture claims you need to have. This is bullshit. If you don't believe me, find a tiny human to make art with and watch creativity come to life. We are literally born with it. What if we changed the rules? What could we accomplish if we simply said, 'Nope, not today' and went about creating the kind of inclusive and creative learning environment we all deserve? A place where we are all recognized for being the writers, artists, and creators we truly are?

I'm sharing these stories and facets of myself with you even though they are not unique. You may even see yourself in some of my stories. I share them here because stories matter. It is how we make connections. It is how we build community. I passionately believe that for you to fully understand this book you need to know who I am and how I got where I am. I want you to see me. How many resources do we read, in particular, scholarly, where we only know a few details about the person behind the words? I wholeheartedly believe research is not only a conversation but a form of creative storytelling. Research is storytelling! By tapping into our own stories, and our own creativity, we can be even better educators than we currently are. We can bring out the best in our students while making space for them to be seen, heard, and valued. This basic premise is the foundation of educating with empathy.

Relationality

Shawn Wilson (2009) writes beautifully in his book *Research is Ceremony: Indigenous Research Methods* that "relationality requires that you know a lot more about me before you can begin to understand my work" (p. 12). For my book to really speak to you, a relationship must be formed between me, the creator, and you, the witness. For this relationship to be impactful, you also need to know and understand the relationship I have with the resources, experiences, and knowledge that have informed me and my work. Relationality is then, quite simply, the relationship I have with my knowledge sources which thereby informs and impacts the relationship I have with you. I am accountable to not only my own relationship to this material but my relationship that will hopefully form with you throughout your spiritual witnessing of this work.

This is my attempt at forming a relationship with you.

My name is Dawn Marie Rogers. My parents were Judy Ann Williams and Don Milton Rogers. Both of my parents grew up in rural Tennessee and relocated outside of Gary, Indiana in the late 1960s. My parents were incredibly young when they married. My mother was 16 years old, and my father was 18 years old. He had just received his draft notice for the Vietnam War and my parents married shortly thereafter. My parents struggled with infertility and finally gave up hope of ever having a child. After trying for a decade, they became pregnant with me. My mother always liked the name Dawn and knew that if she ever had a little girl, she would give her that name. I'm not sure where my middle name came from but what I do know is that most of my southern relatives, including my paternal grandmother, conflated my first and middle name and forever referred to me as Dawn Marie. I hated it. Growing up I hated my name mostly because it was not a popular name, and I could never find it on gift shop mini license plates, buttons, or sticker packs. Not like you can today. I also disliked the fact that my name had only one syllable. I felt it lacked power and agency with only that one syllable to hold it up. I felt this strongly during the first grade when we went around the room, said our names, and clapped our collective hands to our syllables. Mine was a short clap whereas everyone else like Kameron, Cassandra, and Alexander went forever echoing on. I also disliked the last name of Rogers. Mostly because during the 1980s my classmates would tease me and ask if my father was Mr. Rogers from *Mr. Rogers' Neighborhood*. It's amazing what we are made to feel embarrassed and ashamed about when there is absolutely nothing to be embarrassed or ashamed of. In fact, now that I am a mother of a young person, I love *Mr. Rogers' Neighborhood* and the spin-off *Daniel Tiger*. So, yes, my father was Mr. Rogers and no, he was not *that* Mr. Rogers.

Both of my parents were born in small towns in Tennessee which is where almost all my relatives resided, and still do. I do not like Tennessee. From an early age I didn't understand my southern relatives' love for the Confederate flag and their general dislike for folx not white. I didn't have the language at the time but what I was feeling and seeing was racism. I was raised in a Southern Baptist home where my paternal grandfather was a pastor. I never felt a connection to that religion even though I was forced to attend Sunday service until I was eighteen years old even though my father somehow got away with staying at home and working in the garage. The Southern Baptist faith has a lot of sexism, racism, xenophobia, and countless other isms running through its interpretation of the Bible. I wasn't down with the whole idea that as a girl I was to be seen not heard. I wasn't about to participate in what my paternal grandmother called 'witnessing' which was basically jumping all over someone about their religious beliefs while also trying to strongarm and guilt-trip them into accepting Christ as their personal savior. To me, this was not teaching but terrorizing.

I grew up in rural Indiana. When I was 3 years old my parents moved us from Gary to 55 acres of land in Jasper County, Indiana. Growing up I heard the reason was that my father wanted to have more space but in adulthood I realized it was White Flight that drove my parents out of Gary into the exclusively white woods. We had three neighbors on our whole street. I hated growing up in the country. I wanted to be able to ride my bike to visit friends or go hang out at the library or local park. Since we lived a half hour drive to the nearest town in either direction, my childhood was an isolated one where friends had to come to me. I spent a lot of time reading Christopher Pike books and writing bad poetry and short stories. I listened to music and watched my maternal grandmother's 'stories' like *General Hospital*. I grew up in an environment where my grandparents were with me daily. My maternal grandmother lived with us, and my paternal grandparents lived on our property in their own house that my father built for them. Just like he built the house we lived in. He had immense pride in the things he built. Building things to stay rooted meant freedom to him.

Freedom to me looked like a car and as soon as I obtained my driver's license and a running vehicle I was gone. I felt rootless and most of the time lost. My time was spent cruising backroads with my best friend, Barbie, listening to jams and frequenting the local truck stop called *Grandma's Kitchen* where we sat many a late night trying to figure out our lives. Drinking that endless cup of coffee that only nineties truck stops could provide. Sometimes splurging for grilled cheese and fries that we shared. We were always torn as to what direction we should take our lives. What was right? What was happiness? What was anything, really?

Grandma's Kitchen has since been torn down. All the folx that occupied my childhood home are dead. The property was taken back by the bank then sold, gutted, and resold. All evidence that we existed and dreamed there is gone. I am all that remains. Rootless and most of the time lost, I grew up without money. I do want to acknowledge that my family's whiteness protected us from the deeper depths of poverty. For many years, my parents were on food stamps. I have vivid memories of waiting in line outside the local VFW for what I called "Reagan Cheese." Every winter my father would be gifted hams from local businesses that he did electrical work for, and my mother spent countless hours trying to come up with a new way to present us with these hams. *Ham ala regret. Ham with a side of tears. Ham marinated in bad luck and a hard winter. Ham and this is terrible.* I ate enough ham in my childhood to last many lifetimes which is why I won't eat it today.

When I was in elementary school my father was transplanting pine trees alongside the driveway. The top of one of the pine trees broke off and he was going to throw it away, but I begged him to let me plant it. With just a sand shovel, I dug a hole right in front of my backyard playhouse (which was a converted pigsty) and planted my tree. I was so proud of that tree. I suspect that my father came back later and planted it deeper into the ground although he never admitted to it. My tree ended up being the tallest of all the pine trees we planted that day. That tree came to symbolize hope for me. That despite your roots you can grow tall and strong. You can outgrow your surroundings if you reach high enough and far enough. You can move beyond your past, your family legacy, and generational trauma. I was that tree. I am still that tree.

Right before the bank took possession of the property I went back and posed for pictures under my tree. It truly is magnificent. The new owners will never know the symbolism planted there, how those roots are still talking to my roots I laid down here in Massachusetts. That I am still informed by the knowledge it shares with me about strength, resiliency, and spirituality. It stands as a reminder that all things are connected. That we are all connected. Past to present. There and here. Now and then. Before and after. Always and forever.

Perhaps I am not rootless after all.

Why am I telling you all of this? What does any of this have to do with this book? Quite simply, it is everything. It is the beginning. It is how I got where I am today and there is no tangible way to show you who I am and the journey that was laid out before me unless you see a little bit of where I came from. I want you to know me and while we certainly cannot form a true lasting friendship here within these pages, I do hope that we can develop a relationship where you walk away with a real sense of me. I honor that potential relationship by being accountable to this material and the way I present it to you. To know me is to hear my stories. I am my stories. To know our students is to hear their stories. Not stories in the westernized sense that stories are fiction and make-believe but rather stories as pieces of who we are. Those pieces of us that we are capable of putting into words and actions that help build empathy and community, and true knowledge. Academia, specifically in the western world, does all it can to strip us of our humanity, of what makes us us. Academia all but forces us to leave our stories at home and come to the classroom as objectively as possible by stripping the first-person voice from scholarship. But true objectivity is not possible. We are human beings with complex feelings, emotions, and thoughts. We need to embrace our stories, not silence them. We need stories. Our students need stories. The world needs stories. From me, from you, and from our students. I believe that research and scholarship are a conversation, a story, and throughout this book, I hope to show you different ways to engage in this conversation. To share stories. So, let's share space together, here and now, as I tell you stories that I hope will bring you light and love from my most authentic self.

Lineage and Roots

Just as research does not exist in a vacuum neither do my accomplishments. I am blessed with encountering so many wonderful and inspiring folx along my many trips around the sun. Our conversations, interactions, and the sharing of space has helped bring me where I am right now. I can't possibly thank everyone, but I do want to show gratitude to a few individuals. Leanne Spencer, you convinced me to teach my very first information literacy course. Even though I was absolutely terrified I am so glad I took a chance and trusted you. Thank you for seeing something in me I couldn't. May you rest in peace. Mary Alice Ball, you were the first and only professor I encountered in graduate school who really saw and understood my uniqueness. Your encouragement over the years has been a port in various storms and I am forever grateful for your time, wisdom, and friendship. Rex Krajewski, you redefined for me what leadership means. You mentored me with not only professionalism, but empathy and that combination is so often missing from the workplace. Thank you for always listening with an open mind anytime I said, "Okay, so I have an idea." Matt Bejune, thank you for the second chance to interview. Had it not been for that second chance I might not be where I am today. Elizabeth McKeigue, thank you for providing the professional development funds for me to enroll in *Book in 90* which led to this book. Alexandria Peary, I am forever indebted to you for not only encouraging me to send out my poems but for doing so mindfully. Thank you, Gina Capra, for your endless capacity to listen, empathize, and strategize. And of course, for my yearly rune readings that help guide me throughout the year. Nina Clements, thank you for reminding me to use my voice. Saher Selod, thank you for taking the chance to incorporate zines into your sociology course. I learned so much from you and your students. The work they created still moves me today and has set the bar for all classes moving forward. Thank you, Sage Adderley, for opening your heart, home, and family to me with genuine kindness. Thank you for helping me find the roses in my writing. Without your *Book in 90* program, I would have written zero words instead of the 56,000 or so words contained here. To my fellow writers in the *Book in 90* program, I have always seen the bright stars of the night sky but now I know a few of their names. My Witch and Bitch coven, I love each one of you. Thank you for holding space with me, for sharing community, magick, and zines. This group is a true testament to the power of global friendship and feminism. To all the zinesters out there, keep writing and producing zines. The world needs your stories, now more than ever. Thank you to everyone I have traded zines with over the decades and for reading my zines. To my coven at Hauswitch. Thank you for providing the magickal space necessary to do the work I am called to do. Dez "Cookie" Alaniz, my soul cookie and twin flame. Thank you for your wiggles, giggles, dreams, and schemes. *There is magic all around you if I do say so myself.* Barb and John Stahura, thank you for supporting me and believing in me. Mom and Dad, thank you for giving me breath so I could use my voice. Elise, I am so grateful for the time I had with you. So much of the work I do now is because of your short life and tragic death. Barbie Baer, there is not enough space in this book to properly thank you for the last thirty-seven years of best friendship. You are my soulmate, soul sister, and best shoe. So much of who I am today is because of you. I love you. Matt Stahura, you have shown me what "if by sheer will alone" really looks like. Thank you for always pushing me forward and for loving my brain. Olive. Lastly, to Rowan Stahura, my little Squish, my baby. Giving birth to you is the most profound and meaningful contribution I will ever make to this world. I never realized just how deep love could be until I met you. Your magick will move mountains and I am so proud of the light you have already poured over this world. I will forever hold back as much darkness as I can so that you can find your way.

Introduction

What This Book is About

This book is about teaching the whole creative student with elements not normally found inside the classroom. *Educating with Empathy* is a framework for teaching and instruction that incorporates storytelling, spirituality, critical creativity, and social justice. It's about shifting proximities of power to make space for the students in the room. Inside this book, you will find woven throughout my story, instruction ideas, community-building techniques, and critical creativity activities to use in the classroom, wherever your classroom may be. You will get ideas on how you can use the educating with empathy framework to build out your own practice.

Each chapter is broken up into the five essential elements of life: earth, air, fire, water, and spirit. After each element I list what it provides for us and/or draws out of us. One is not more important than the other and for empathy to develop, these five elements must be present. Academia currently divides our spiritual selves from our teaching and learning identities because so many of our institutions are run like businesses instead of places of creativity and inquiry. To be clear, spirituality is not the same thing as religion. I am in no way advocating for bringing religion into the classroom as I firmly stand by the separation of church and state. What I am advocating for is allowing spirituality to take up space in our teaching. We are all spiritual beings. It is what connects us to the earth, to ourselves, and to each other.

> More specifically, spirituality is 'about a sense of wholeness, healing, and interconnectedness of all things...it is about moving toward this greater sense of one's deepest spirit, or more authentic identity" (Tisdell & Tolliver, 2003, p. 374).

It's what allows for empathy, a way of truly seeing and connecting with other folx. We cannot be truly empathetic if we are not utilizing the necessary elements of life. There is spirit all around you. You don't need to believe in spirituality because it exists already without your belief. All I ask is that you read with an open mind and heart. If you do this, I guarantee you will shift your perspective on teaching, creativity, expertise, and research. Some of the things I talk about might be unconventional or far out or nonsensical. Take what you can carry now and come back for the rest later. I'll be waiting.

Empathy takes courage[1]. I'm glad you are here.

Who This Book Is For

This book is for YOU. I come to you as a research and instruction librarian, a lifelong zinester, a feminist, a queer activist, a mother, a best friend, a partner, and an artist. I am an educator at heart. A teacher of things, a dreamer of dreams, and a weaver of webs. I imagine if you have picked up this book you identify as one or a few of these things too. When I sat down to write this book, I envisioned librarians of all sorts engaged with the content and making notes in the margins. (Yes, I am one of those folx who love marginalia). I wholeheartedly believe that anyone who finds themselves in an educator (and yes, librarians are educators) role, be it through libraries, K-12 education, community organizing, non-profit spaces, and perhaps capitalistic realms, will find something here that can be easily implemented to create more empathetic and critically creative environments. You are definitely multi-faceted with intersecting identities so when I address the reader, know that I am really addressing YOU. Whomever YOU are. I hope throughout this book that I can build a rapport with you and that you learn not just about what I do but why I do it and who I am through the work I do. The more folx who commit to this kind of work, the more inclusive and empathetic our learning spaces will be. We need these spaces now more than ever. We need more white folx to do this work. I come to this book with certain privileges, and I plan to use them in whatever way I can to build the kind of spaces that teach holistically. Classrooms are just places of creation and I'm ready to create a more empathic and socially-just teaching and learning environment.

---

1 The root of the word courage is cor—the Latin word for heart. In one of its earliest forms, the word courage meant "To speak one's mind by telling all one's heart (Brown, 2010, p. 12).

Chapter 1

Spirit
Connection, Balance, Space

First you recover it then you reclaim it.

Education is a basic human right and should be accessible to all folx regardless of who they are and where they come from. Education is liberation and a pathway to not only understanding the world but creating lasting change in it. I became a librarian because I am passionate about education and the fundamental role librarianship plays in the education of others. To paraphrase philosopher Paulo Freire's *Pedagogy of the Oppressed* (1970), education is the emancipation of oppressed groups. Librarianship encourages freedom of speech, protects and promotes intellectual freedom, and provides avenues for interacting, remixing, and creating information and resources. I remain a librarian because of the need for librarianship in social justice movements. Information is not neutral and how we interact with and understand the role of information is crucial for creating equitable and inclusive spaces inside and outside academia. Education is social justice. My teaching philosophy and style emerged from watching students (like me) not see themselves in their research. I've worked at R1 institutions, state universities, community colleges, for-profits, and women-centered liberal arts colleges and the one thing that all these places have in common are students who feel completely disconnected and disembodied from the research process. So many students are living with experiences that reinforce that there is no connection between their daily lives and their academic learning. There is a myriad of reasons why, from systematic oppression, bias language in catalogs and databases, false narratives, and histories (yes, even in libraries) and the way expertise is pigeon-holed in western colonizer white men's ideas and research. bell hooks (1994) writes in the opening of her book *Teaching to Transgress* that "knowledge was suddenly information only. It had no relation to how one lived, behaved. It was no longer connected to antiracist struggle" (p. 3).

Our education system and libraries were never meant to be fully inclusive, yet we often pretend they were. These systems that are still in place are a testament to who we let in but more importantly who we keep out, whether we are consciously aware of it or not. These systems prevent so many of our students from really connecting to the creative and transformative processes that research can encompass. The truth is research is meaningful when it makes a difference to our communities, and we provide a disservice to a huge population of learners when we do not provide space for building communities of practice inside and outside the classroom. During the pandemic so many of us grappled with *what is time* and came to understand that time is just a construct. I fully understand that most educators spend a finite amount of time with their students. As a librarian, I am all too familiar with one-shot instruction sessions, where I come into a classroom to discuss research strategies and ways in which library resources can help. Essentially, I am presenting *all the things* that students must know before embarking on their research journey in 50 minutes or less. After 15+ years of this type of instruction, I have come to realize that the most important thing I want students to walk away with is the ability to see themselves in their research. The truth is, this can be accomplished in a short amount of time if done well and consistently.

I am a spiritual being and bring my whole self to the classroom just like our students bring their whole selves, even the messy and ill-informed facets. I am constantly evolving like everyone else and so each time I enter the classroom I bring the newest, most updated version of myself. This along with my teaching has value. Bringing my whole self, even those imperfect older versions allows me to practice what I call *educating with empathy*. I know how important it is to make space for critical learning and more importantly critical unlearning. I am transparent about what I know and what I don't know. Being honest about the messiness of research, the writing process, and creativity in general means being transparent. This transparency builds trust which builds community. Our students cannot trust a process that looks polished and perfect from the get-go. As a creative person, my art is not precious. What I mean by this is that I am always learning, always growing, and expanding. I am willing to throw out what doesn't work and make space for different ideas and processes. By sharing how research and creative processes look, it gives students the permission to stumble, make mistakes, make numerous attempts, and ultimately create something meaningful.

For full transparency, I did not just sit down one day and write this entire book. In truth, I have been writing this book in various small increments (articles, notes, conversations with colleagues) over the past decade. An opportunity arose which I could not pass up; the opportunity to write this book in a structured way with mentorship support. It has not been easy. It has not always been fun. There have been days that I wanted to walk away from this project and never look at it again. There were days that I felt like an imposter with nothing new or meaningful to say. There were days when my inner critic, who I call Chad, laughed at me for even attempting this endeavor. But I kept going. Meaningful research, creations, etc. are about movement. If we are moving, we are not technically stuck. Throughout the book, I will provide this kind of transparency so that neither of us is disillusioned about what the research, writing, and creative processes look like.

This same movement applies to my teaching. I learn from students daily. From classrooms to consultations, students bring their questions, insights, personalities, and curiosities with them. They also bring their expertise. I realize that the words *expertise* and *students* rarely go together in academia but to teach holistically, we need to recognize and make space for students' expertise. While they are not experts in their field of study nor in the courses they are enrolled in, they are experts of their own lived experiences. These lived experiences are constantly shaping the way they interact and react to information. If we want to teach with empathy, we must make space for those lived experiences in the classroom because those narratives have value, just as my teaching and knowledge have value. My teaching and their learning are in dialogue with one another which allows me to modify the way I present information based on where the students are and what they need in the moment. I teach to the students, not my expectations. Building community is essential to practicing empathy and I believe education and librarianship need more empathy. If I believe that education is the emancipation of the oppressed, then I must find avenues to achieve that every time I walk into a classroom and every time, I encounter a student.

My most essential role as an educator is to spiritually witness and not in the Southern Baptist way I mentioned earlier. I define spiritual witnessing as being authentic and fully present in the exchange of ideas. It is sharing the stage and allowing students to be active participants in their learning. It is active listening and refraining from the need to fix and correct. I spiritually witness and respond to their inquiries and creations. I offer guidance and alternative ways of assessing and understanding information. I guide them through the uncertainty, confusion, and fear that is often part of the research process to a place of embodied learning and knowledge. This is a facet of my career that I do not take lightly, and it is an honor and a privilege to be in this unique position of medium and listener. For me to truly and fully listen, I must leave my ego at the door. True learning and the generation of new ideas cannot exist if the ego is taking up space. Once I check my ego, I am fully present for my students in mind, body, and spirit. Without the ego, I can be empathetic to not only their struggles but their triumphs. I can admit when I do not know something or have all the answers. I can say with honesty that we will find the answers together as research is not just a journey but a conversation that does not exist inside a vacuum. That the work we do is in conversation with their learning goals and objectives and if we are creating movement, we are open to new ideas and ways of knowing.

It is in the unexpected moments in the classroom and in research consultations that real transformation happens. As an educator, I see the visible shift in consciousness as things come into focus for students. Structure and learning objectives are obviously important (not only to curriculum mapping but to instructional design as well), but structure must be partnered with playfulness and creativity for truly deep learning to happen. I am open to that unknown and leave room for my instruction to take a different path once I know where the students are and what specific obstacles stand in their way from fully embracing the research process. This openness to the unknown is one of the intentions I set before walking into the classroom. Intentionality is one of the most important aspects of any type of work whether that be professional, personal, and/or creative. All creative endeavors which include research begin with an idea, but it is the intention to DO something with that idea that is powerful. The doing is where educators live. We guide students from their idea through the doing and into the finished project. We are mediums that provide translations between realms of experience and realms of knowledge. Without intention setting, we are forever stuck in the thinking phase, generating idea after idea without any forward movement. Remember, if we are creating movement, we are open to new ways of learning, seeing, and being.

As a deeply spiritual person, I know how far out this sounds and believe me, if I had not witnessed these transformations with students firsthand, I would chalk this up to some new age nonsense. I'm sharing these stories with you because they work. Real and deep transformations do happen. I've seen them. I've actually been one of those transformed. One specific way I can see my transformations is through the writing of positionality statements. Creating yearly positionality statements provides the chance to look over what we have (un)learned in the last year. I will talk specifics about this later but for now these statements help bring into focus how we approach our work, the intersections that our identities meet, and how those identities play out in the way we teach and interact with students. Some of our positions are static. For example, I cannot change my race or my age but my position on certain situations or learning objectives do change over time, as they should. Writing a yearly positionality statement helps me see where I have been and where I am going so I can best serve my students and community members. Positionality statements are not just for professionals. They are great exercises for students as well. What better way to really understand their research, their interactions and hidden biases with information, and how who they are affects how they perceive and represent their work. The power of this cannot be overstated. I've seen students uncover truths about themselves that they never knew were there by writing about the intersections of their identities. I've seen scholarly work improve when students get the chance to critically think about how they know what they know and the implications of it.

All of this is to say that who we are, including our spiritual self, provides a connection to the research process, balance within ourselves and with each other, and creates a space for deep learning and transformation. I'm over the idea that we leave our personal selves at the classroom door. Yes, leave the ego because it gets in the way of empathy and connection but bring our whole selves. To do anything less is a disservice to not only you but the students waiting inside the classroom to learn. There are plenty of other spaces in academia that will ask us to disassociate and disembody to fit the mold. (Any tenure track folx reading this?) As June Jordan writes in *Poetry for the People: A Revolutionary Blueprint* (1995, 7),

"I had become part of an academic community where you could love school because school did not have to be something apart from, or in denial of, your own life [...]. School could become, in fact, a place where students learned about the world and then resolved, collectively and creatively to change it!" (p. 7).

The classroom is our space. Let us claim it as such and set our intentions to teach with empathy.

Spirit Activities

Lineage and Roots

No one achieves success without the help of others. Empathy asks us to acknowledge those who have helped us along our life's journey. In every facet of our life, we have had folx who mentored us, cared for us, spiritually witnessed us, created with us, and dismantled oppression with us. One way to practice empathy is to write out our lineage and roots. Who are the folx who have carried us when we needed it? Whose shoulders did we lean on, cry on in our darkest moments? Who laughed with us when we were at our silliest? Writing out our lineage and roots is a powerful activity that connects us to our past and provides a tangible cord for us to follow into our future. While you do not have to share your lineage and roots publicly, I will say there is something powerful about letting folx know how they have impacted you and the work you do. Even if the folx in your life know how important they are to you, having a reminder never hurts anyone.

The Work

Reflection Questions

- Do you see yourself as an educator? Why or why not?
- How do you define *education* and in what ways do you attempt to dismantle oppression in the classroom?
- How do you feel about the role of spiritual *witness*? Does the term make you uncomfortable?

Reflection Activities

- Write your lineage and roots and consider showing it to some folx who inspired you. Be open to the ways in which this exercise will create not only conversations but opportunities for learning and growth.
- Create your own definition of *education* and apply it to the work that you do. Think about the areas in your professional life where you might be falling short by your definition. Consider writing out ways you can stretch. There are areas in which you are excelling (I am sure of it), and I invite you to celebrate those achievements.

Chapter 2

Educating with Empathy framework

When I truly hear you, I know you.

I am fortunate to have a creative partner, dreamer, and schemer in all things academic. Dez Alaniz and I spend a lot of time talking about our creative processes and instruction methodologies and the ways they intersect in the classroom. I am so thankful for the space we have carved out for us to critically and creatively talk about the work we do and, more importantly, the work we want to do. Every type of institution has its red tape and bureaucratic bloat. Every place of education has folx who are just going through the motions lecturing at a room full of uninspired and half-asleep students. Every place has folx in power who are resistant to change and real transformation. Every space of learning has folx who hide behind biases, systemic oppression, and White privilege. Over the course of my professional career, I have learned how to set tiny fires that allow the kind of (destruction) instruction I want and need to do without burning down the whole establishment (even if it really should burn). One afternoon Dez and I were talking about one-shots and how often we hear that x or y cannot be done because of time constraints, and I shared at length about how I had seen transformations happen inside the classroom with activities that don't take a super long time. I thought to myself, *I should really be writing this down.* It was then that I started to gather all my instruction notes and ideas into one place. What I gathered became the body of this book. What made the leap between talking about my ideas and writing my ideas is the act of spiritual witnessing. Dez and I are always witnessing each other. We have a relationship built upon empathy with allows us to truly see and hear each other. Through the act of witnessing, I can clearly see how connected we are to the world, to each other, to knowledge, and to our creativity. As Tricia Hersey (2022) beautifully writes in her book *Rest is Resistance: A Manifesto,* we are taught to believe that we accomplish our goals by ourselves. "This is false because there is a spiritual dimension that exists in all things and in everything we do" (p. 18). Our lives are one big spiritual practice. If we take the time to really listen, we will hear the myriad of voices that connect us to each other and the earth. If we open ourselves to the message we receive, we will find our own authentic voice by spiritually witnessing others.

The title of the chapter is *Educating with Empathy Framework.* So, what exactly is empathy? At the core, it recognizes and values students' lived experiences and makes space for where students are in the moment. It's moving beyond the role of teacher to a role as (spiritual) witness. Remember, witnessing means actively listening inside the classroom with our whole selves, which includes our spiritual selves. It is teaching and learning holistically. I started referring to my teaching style as *educating with empathy* in 2019 to describe the culmination of all my teaching and experiences in a variety of settings. This framework is informed and built upon four guiding elements: information spectrums / spirituality / social justice / and critical creativity. Together these elements create empathy. The following chapters will go into more detail about what each of these guiding elements is and what they can look like inside the classroom and beyond. Each chapter ends with some reflection questions and some critical creativity exercises for you to try out. We cannot ask our students to do something we are not willing to do ourselves. As bell hooks (1994) writes in *Teaching to Transgress,* "professors who expect students to share confessional narratives but who are themselves unwilling to share are exercising power in a manner that could be coercive" (p. 21). If we want to educate with empathy, we have to participate.

What do I mean when I say to practice empathy? Empathy is the combination of self-actualization and the ability to see, understand, and feel another person's point of view. It is being able to understand their positionality and move forward from a place of spiritual witnessing. Empathy does not come easily for a lot of folx so practicing empathy daily is crucial to fully embracing it as a framework. Empathy is not sympathy. To lovingly paraphrase Brené Brown (2010) from her TED talk *The Power of Vulnerability,* sympathy is feeling sorry for someone without any real connection or movement forward. Sympathy is *I hear you and I feel bad but there is nothing I can do.* Empathy says, *"I hear you. I see you. I witness your story and I am going to allow myself to feel your story and emotions and make a true and meaningful connection with you. You are not alone.* Empathy takes courage. In Brené Brown's (2010) book *The Gifts of Imperfection* she reminds us that the root of the word courage is *cor*—the Latin word for heart. "In one of its earliest forms, the word courage meant *to speak one's mind by telling all one's heart*" (p. 12). So, what makes empathy so powerful? When we truly connect to another person, transformation happens both within ourselves and the space between each person. The space between is liminal where new ideas are born, new ways of being and thinking emerge, and where shifts in consciousness occur. Liminal simply means that we are between things, it is not this or that yet. When we enter this liminal space, true learning can happen.

Practicing empathy is not an easy feat but I believe it is necessary to not only effectively teach but to practice true inclusivity within the classroom. All of us want to do the best for our students, to form real connections with them, and to provide them with the tools of curiosity and creativity to set fire to the world. Besides wanting to be the absolute best educators we can be, I believe practicing empathy provides practitioners the ability and space to embody social justice principles such as active listening, decentering dominant narratives, and recognizing proximities of power. Empathy makes space for different definitions of expertise knowing that expertise does exist outside of traditional forms of scholarship. We create the vital movement past the inherent bias towards scholarly, peer-reviewed sources and make room for other types of valuable knowledge.

Empathy allows for scholarship to truly be a conversation, a story, by recognizing that we all enter an ongoing scholarly conversation no matter the subject of our research. Through empathy, we provide students the opportunity to seek out the conversation and discover its shape, path, and history and how they, the student, fit into it. Most importantly empathy allows us to embody the truth that all information has value. Imagination is information. Dreams, memories, and inspiration are all valid forms of information. More than just traditional forms of knowledge have value depending on what you need the information to do. By practicing empathy, we create space for true scholarship and inquiry to take place.

The Work

Reflection Questions

- What are your initial thoughts about the *educating with empathy* framework? (Be honest).

- Have you ever considered the role empathy can play in your role as an educator?

- Can you think of instances where you have practiced empathy?

Chapter 3

Earth
Foundation, Building Blocks, Grounded

I am rooted in transition.

Information exists on a spectrum. From scholarly articles to fake news, all information exists somewhere on the spectrum. What determines its importance is what we need from the resource; what we need it to do. There is no perfect resource. Every piece of information has its place. Some resources are better suited for particular types of research than others. Knowing where information exists on the spectrum guides students in selecting the best resources for their informational needs. All information has value, even fake news depending on what they need the information to do. If a student is researching the negative impact of fake news on the general population's willingness to social distance during the pandemic, fake news would be extremely valuable to them. I want the classroom to provide space to teach students how to discern what resources are valuable for their specific research needs. The resources change all the time as information is fluid. Information spectrums consider intention. What we intend to do with a specific resource is as important as the resource itself.

Authority exists on the information spectrum as well. Different types of research need specific kinds of experts. Authority and expertise come in all shapes and sizes from scholarly articles, dreams, professional credentials, intuition, trade journals, spiritual beliefs, academic blogs, and gut instincts. Not all authority and expertise are found within the very narrow western colonizer viewpoint of what types of information have value. Information spectrums make space for all ways of knowing and being. They provide opportunities to critically engage with them at the right time.

We are constantly (un)learning. We can be a novice at one thing and an expert at another, often simultaneously. We move along information spectrums as we learn and grow. Information spectrums allow space for students to be experts. Everyone has expertise. We all have expertise and authority over our lived experiences. True learning comes from that place of expertise and expands as we broaden our view of information spectrums. Our lived experiences are our true place of knowing. When we ask students to consistently place authority exclusively outside of themselves, they have less control over their own learning, creativity, and discovery. We cannot be afraid of students claiming their expertise in the classroom because when we are, we shut down an opportunity for empathy.

I hate the term *information literacy* because it positions the learner inside a scarcity mindset. The fastest way to shut down a learning opportunity is to use the phrase *information literacy* with someone. For years, I tried the term *critical information literacy* but it still felt inadequate. I now use the term *information spectrums* to explain the same concepts. Semantics matter. Biased subject headings and classification systems have proven this. Spectrums are a concept we understand and if we can understand it, we can be comfortable using it.

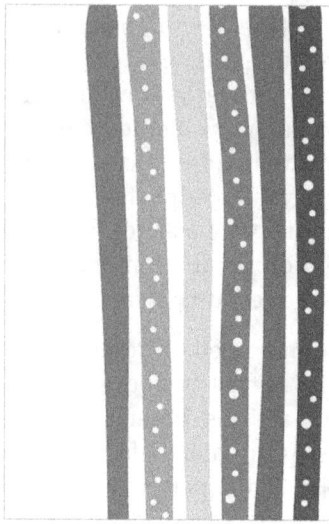

Expertise is vetted. Expertise is earned. There is a huge spectrum of knowledge and each of us can be a novice at one thing and an expert at another.

Along information spectrums are parallel stories which help us understand and humanize our research. Parallel stories provide a window into lived experiences and a doorway to empathy. These stories are found within zines, community activism, patient narratives, illness stories, diaries, art, music, and other forms of creative expression. It's important to read scholarly articles and/or scientific papers on a topic to get a grasp of the subject matter but imagine how much richer the experience would be if a parallel story was also provided. I've worked with students over the years on topics in every discipline and I can tell you that no matter what the subject area, parallel stories make a huge difference in the way students approach and engage with their research. They get the opportunity to witness their research and come at it with empathy as opposed to the level of detachment we insist makes good research. There is no *I* in research although truth be told, we never go anywhere without ourselves, even in our research. I get that research is supposed to be objective when it comes to writing scholarly resources, but we all have emotions, unconscious biases, and experiences that shape the way we see and move through the world. Of course, these facets of ourselves make it into our research whether we are aware of it or not. The mere idea that there is no *I* in research is a fallacy, and an unattainable goal. What we are really saying is that we don't want to hear the students anywhere in their research. We want them as neutral as possible as if neutrality was even an option.

With research, something is lost through the researcher's gaze. Stories and narratives are filtered through the person collecting, analyzing, and interpreting the data. Maybe for the most part that is okay, but I think there are situations where firsthand accounts are needed. Consider the research published on marginalized communities. Their experiences are not conveyed to the reader as firsthand accounts but instead filtered through the researcher's gaze into interpretations, outcomes, etc. We lose a vital connection to the group being observed and as a result, we lose the chance to experience real empathy. When researchers outside of marginalized groups conduct studies and research on those communities, it is done through a westernized colonizer lens that does not represent the lived experiences and knowledge of those communities. Countless studies are conducted that position marginalized groups as less than by comparing their worth to Western ideals and knowledge systems.

Let's also consider patient narratives and their unique relationships with the medical community, their illnesses, disabilities, etc.

Patient stories are crucial for building not only empathy with those who live outside the scope of the experience but in building community with folx who are seeking solidarity. It is one thing to read a research article on the complications of chemotherapy on patients with chronic obstructive pulmonary disease (COPD) but it's another to read a personal narrative account of a patient sitting inside the statistics. Not only do we humanize our research, but we hold on to the vital connections of real people with a real stake in the results. I worked with a student who was researching to see if anxiety around perfectionism was linked to eating disorders in female college students. She was happy with the scholarly content we found. Instead of ending the consultation there, I asked if she was interested in reading a few zines written by college students living with eating disorders and anxiety. She had never heard of zines and was super curious about them. I stressed that while she probably couldn't use them as scholarly sources in her bibliography, she could use them as background information. At the end of the semester, she returned the zines to me, and we had an in-depth conversation about the impact of zines on her research. What was most profound was how she could see, hear, and feel how the zine authors' lives were impacted by anxiety and their eating disorder. She understood that actual patients were observed in the research articles she read, but she admitted she didn't think too deeply about who they were or why they were involved in the study. Zines allowed her to write a more authentic and impactful research paper because of the parallel stories.

Another student was writing a research paper on the ecological and environmental impact of hurricanes on Haiti. I asked the student if they were open to reading a zine written about the devastation Haiti experienced after Hurricane Matthew in 2016. A few weeks later I met with the student again and they thanked me for lending them the zine. Not only was the information relevant to their topic but the images used throughout the zine were compelling. What really resonated with the student was the note at the very end of the zine that explained that all the images were taken by the author's grandmother while she was walking through her neighborhood. This small note had the most profound impact on the student because it grounded their research. Statistics represent actual people, a fact that is often lost on students when reading research articles. Seeing those images of devastation in the zine and then finding out who took them rooted the student in their research in a way no other resource could. Parallel stories matter and the more we advocate for their inclusion in student research, the more well-rounded and empathetic our students will be. Empathy will go with them out into the world, their communities, and their relationships, partnerships, and work environments. This is how college-level research can have a lasting impact on the students. Real and lasting change happens through relationships.

I want to take a moment and talk about how this realization that we are not just statistics really hit home for me. I'd been an academic librarian for a few years and was well-accustomed to teaching instruction sessions, demystifying what peer-reviewed articles were and how to read them. At the time, most students were told (by their professors and me) to skip the methodology section. For the types of research the students were doing, the abstract, introduction, discussion, and conclusion were more than enough to satisfy the assignment requirements. But that wasn't really true. One evening I was reading a zine called *Cocoa/Puss #2* where the author talked about how inherently racist our healthcare systems are and how this rhetoric places the blame on black folx instead of the systems themselves. At one point, the author writes, "there is so much racism in public health and so many health disparities. I just want you to know that everything you read is not a FACT, ok? Statistics don't explain the whole story" (Cocoa/Puss Zine, n.d.). Let me say this again. Statistics don't explain the whole story. Boom. There it was, staring me right in the face. I had inadvertently perpetuated racist evaluation methods by not advocating for students to read the methodology section. Now I tell students that the methodology section is the heart of the research paper. This section contains more than just statistics. Sometimes there are people there. Sometimes there are people missing. There is always a story buried beneath and within the data.

Our academic institutions are governed by capitalism which disregards experiential knowledge as a form of expertise and authority.

For many folx it does not matter that they have expertise through years of knowing and doing because unless they have papers (degrees, certificates, etc.), it is not considered valid. Capitalism states that unless we put ourselves into debt both financially and emotionally, our voices, experiences, and innate knowledge won't matter. I'll use myself as an example. I've written creatively my whole life. I have also been an artist in some form throughout my time on this planet. Now whether I felt comfortable calling myself an artist or a writer is another story. I have a Bachelor of Arts degree in creative writing, an Associate of Applied Science in business management, and a master's in library and information sciences. I've written and published zines since the 90s and have written and published scholarly articles and book chapters in the past decade. I've had the pleasure of creating and teaching my own undergraduate courses in information literacy and personal narrative writing. I've created and taught courses through Indiana University, the American Library Association and the Library Juice Academy on critical information literacy, using pop culture in instruction, and zines as scholarship. I've led workshops and given presentations and webinars on all of these topics and more. What I am not is qualified to teach creative writing, art, or any combination of the two without another degree—the Master of Fine Arts. It doesn't matter what I have done or how well received that work was. All folx see on my CV is that I do not have an MFA. Experiential knowledge won't get me to the first round of interviews and I'm white.

I bring up race because I, as a white person, have an advantage over folx of color. These truths are felt harder within marginalized communities, especially among Black women as the Cocoa zine highlighted. Our educational institutions are built upon systemic oppression, and it will take the dismantling of White supremacy in this country for our educational systems to be equitable. From K-12 onward, our current education system thrives on promoting Whiteness while consistently coming up with new ways to keep nonwhite folx from obtaining the same education. One effective way of invalidating nonwhite folx is the 'consensus' on what is research, what is knowledge, and who should have access to it. Our cultural and spiritual knowledge is valid and continuously shapes the way we move through the world, yet it does not have an academic impact in terms of where we are positioned along information spectrums. To bring this knowledge into the classroom and have it validated by the academy would mean burning down centuries of white male dominance. For our Indigenous students, cultural and spiritual knowledge play a significant role in how they interact with education and the systems of information. We, as a western colonizer country, have completely different ways of describing, archiving, writing, and organizing information that position whiteness as the default, but we need to include other ways of knowing to engage in deep leaning. Making space for experiential knowledge in the classroom is imperative if we are to dismantle the power white supremacy has. The inclusion of other ways of knowing allows empathy to expand and evolve.

> "When such incorporation of other ways of knowing occurs in the context of community, people connect…and are often moved to social action and transformation on behalf of themselves and their own cultural groups or as allies to another cultural group" (Tisdell & Tolliver, 2003, p. 371).

The research process is a story. At the heart of research is a story despite how it is wrapped up and presented to us. This is one of the reasons I chose to start this book with the story of how I arrived at educating with empathy. My story is necessary to not only build a connection but to share the messy process of writing. Imagine how approachable research would be if we talked openly about why we research and how the actual process goes. When we demystify the research process, students are not so intimidated by it. I meet students weekly who are riddled with fear and anxiety around doing research. The most intimidating part for the student is searching for information. I know how hard research can be and I also know how fun and life-changing it can be. I tell students that I didn't wake up one day knowing how to effectively research. It takes time and with practice, anyone can do it. The research process is riddled with mistakes, pitfalls, missteps, and misinformation. These issues are essential to understanding a topic. Scientific research is built upon false starts and mistakes. We need those missteps to know what doesn't work so we can see what does.

Having transparency in the research process is critical for student engagement. Most of us know how to find information. In fact, we find too much information. What I bring to the research conversation are specific tricks and techniques that can elevate the work that students are already doing. I add to their unique skill sets so that they have more than one tool to use. I have seen positive results by doing the work alongside the students. I used to over-prep before instruction sessions. I selected a topic, generated my keywords, and search strings ahead of time so that when in front of students, my search was seamless. I knew not only how many results my search yielded but which article I would use for class discussion. While this alleviated some of my anxiety around teaching, it increased the students' anxiety. What they saw was me going into a database with several keywords and getting usable results on my first try. It was if I had screamed, "Look how easy it is!" They only saw part of the research process. I hid the time I spent brainstorming a topic, searching for information, playing around with keywords. You know, the bulk of what searching is about. No wonder students were convinced they couldn't research and were too incompetent to learn how. I no longer prep my sessions beyond basic outlining.

If I want students to take risks, and enter the unknown territory of researching, I must be willing to do it myself in front of the classroom. There is no other way. I genuinely want to lead with empathy, so I must take the same risks. What's the worst that can happen? I think up a topic and find nothing on it. Been there. Chances are so have the students. I find too much information or irrelevant information? We have all experienced this. Empathy is about being courageous and while we might not think that searching in databases takes courage, I believe that anything we do that pushes us outside our comfort circles takes courage. I want students to actively listen and participate, so I must give them something worth listening to. These small tweaks in my teaching have been the building blocks to transforming the way I interact with research, information spectrums and students. Taking risks ground me in the present and there is no better time to create real and lasting connections.

Earth Activities

Information Spectrums

Creating information spectrums is an extremely helpful way for students to understand the fluidity of information. All resources have value and when our students understand this concept, they can become more effective in evaluating the sources they find. Information spectrums can be general like the one I created below, or they can be discipline specific. They can be created by you or assigned to students as a project to complete. Spectrums can be designed in a myriad of ways and encouraging creative freedom will bring to light the diverse ways we understand and interact with information sources.

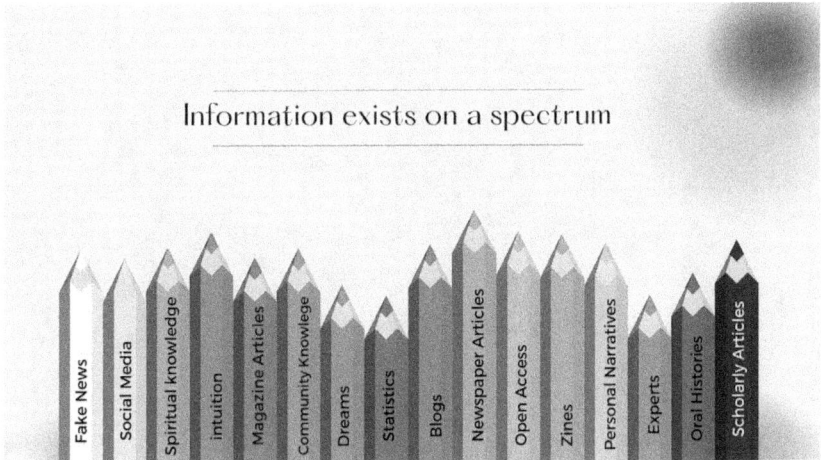

Figure 1 Image by Dawn Stahura

The Work

Reflection Questions

- How do you frame expertise in your discipline or subjects that you teach?
- How do you feel about the term *information literacy?*
- Have you ever considered that information exists on a spectrum? How could this idea be adapted into your teaching?
- Where are you an expert? Where are you a novice?

Reflection Activity

- Create an information spectrum for yourself. Think about the information sources you interact with and where they might fall along the spectrum.
- Create something (a piece of writing, painting, song, etc.) using your own expertise. Center your lived experiences and draw from that wealth of knowledge.

Chapter 4

Act up evaluation method

Let's unpack that.

Like most librarians, I struggle with finding time in one-shot instruction sessions to address evaluating sources. Because of the amount of material I have to cover, I'm lucky if I spend more than five minutes helping students make sense of the information they find. The truth is, evaluating information should be its own class. The last five years alone are enough to warrant 12 or so weeks unpacking what misinformation, disinformation, and propaganda are. Even the 90-minute webinars I teach on fighting back against fake news are only a brief overview of the topic. Evaluating information is social justice work. We have a social and ethical obligation to create, evaluate, and disseminate information that is accurate. None of us live inside a vacuum. Just like I have folx I follow and trust the content they put out, someone else follows me and trusts my posts. I am not infallible. I admit that I have shared information on social media that was inaccurate. We all have. It's easy to do because we don't always take the time to fact-check the things we share. But we should. I want students to care about the process of sharing information and the impact misinformation has on their scholarship, communities, livelihoods, and our democracy. With only a few minutes to talk about evaluating sources, how could I tie evaluating with social justice? How could I stress just how important evaluating information truly is?

I was over the CRAAP (currency, relevance, authority, accuracy, and purpose) evaluation method even though I understood how witty and memorable the acronym was. I felt strongly that the method was missing a social justice piece. Our political climate in 2017 equated *news I don't like or agree with* to fake news from our highest members of government. To me, this opened the door to the kind of activism students and educators could walk through. Running parallel was the fallacy that libraries had been and currently were neutral. Libraries were never neutral (no institution is) and did their fair share of oppressing folx. In 2016 I taught my first Information Sources and Services graduate course and was angry over the whitewashing of library history and reference services. Students needed the true history to understand that library neutrality is a lie. After that semester, I expanded the material I was required to use to include articles and other sources that addressed the role libraries and librarians play in the oppression of marginalized folx. Not fully satisfied, I began looking at what else I could push against. Throughout the course, I incorporated zines written by librarians that illustrated what the reality of librarianship is not just the idea of it. I encouraged students to find their own counternarratives and challenge the course rhetoric. If they couldn't fight against this in the classroom, how would they outside of it? Through the teaching of this course, I realized that pushing against dominant narratives and publishing privilege needed to be addressed not only in the classroom but in the way we evaluate information. We had to address not just who has access to information but also who has the privilege to publish that information. I also had to bring bias into the evaluation conversations if I wanted to highlight how we all have biases. There is no such thing as unbiased. I needed a method that not only addressed these specific aspects but could be taught to everyone, not just library science students. This is how the ACT UP evaluation method was born.

Each letter of ACT UP represents a specific facet of the evaluation process. The "A" represents *author,* but it is more than just who wrote a resource. Students are asked to consider the author's intention in creating the piece and to investigate if any conflict of interest exists between the author and subject matter. The "C" represents *currency.* Beyond merely noting when something was published, *currency* requires students to consider when something was uploaded, retweeted, or shared. Often students assume that when something is shared on social media it also indicates when it was created. This is not always true. These dates matter. The "T" represents *truth.* Here is where semantics matter. How something is framed has impact on its validity. Where something is published might not always be the best indicator of truth as we have seen peer review articles retracted over conflicts of interests, poor statistical analysis and outright deception in the reporting of the supposed results. The "U" represents *unbiased* with the caveat that nothing and no one is unbiased. Asking students how they feel about their research and the topic they selected helps them uncover any unconscious biases they may hold that will ultimately impact the way they research and use the information they find. Lastly, the "P" stands for *privilege* not just in who gets published and where but who has access to resources, how paywalls affect their ability to interact with expertise. This is also an invitation to dive deep into the methodology section and look beyond data points and statistics to see real lives, whether they are human or non-human.

I spent an absurd amount of time trying to come up with an acronym. It needed to be something memorable, recognizable, and tied to social justice. I chose ACT UP because it encompassed all that and created classroom dialogue around social justice movements. I chose the acronym to pay homage to the ACT UP (AIDS Coalition to Unleash Power) movement. I can count on one hand how many times a student knows that ACT UP is a movement and this evaluation method is an opportunity to talk about it. Many students think activism is one and done. Like how the AIDS crisis ended in the 1980s, or that Rosa Parks' refusal to give up her seat was planned in an afternoon. Social justice movements take time but that's hard to imagine in a world where we have access to information and entertainment 24/7. The name ACT UP provides context for students and situates their learning in the broader world of information creation and sharing.

In 2017 I did a soft launch during an instruction session for a first-year writing seminar. The students were writing a critical annotated bibliography. The professor and I had spoken about the ACT UP evaluation method, and he wanted the students to use it, specifically to address privilege in their annotations. During the same semester, I designed and taught a course through the American Library Association on critical information literacy and used the ACT UP method in an assignment. Since both sets of students in the classes were asking how I created the method, I knew it was time to write about it. In 2018 I submitted an article to the *College & Research Libraries News*. Instead of a full-length article, I was given a short *The Way I See It* column. While I was happy to share my evaluation method with others, I was disappointed it did not include the backstory I am sharing here because stories matter. I felt that if folx knew how I arrived at ACT UP, it would strengthen my argument for its use in evaluating sources. Since 2017, I have tweaked it in response to not only our information hellscape but from the feedback from those who have adopted its use. I am humbled when someone teaches my method. I appreciate all the requests to copy and adapt my Libguide on ACT UP. I too, teach with this method inside and outside the classroom and have seen the quality of student evaluations of information greatly improve.

For me, this method is not just an academic checklist for sources but a form of activism itself. Evaluating sources is activism. Evaluating sources is social justice work and the more I can stress this upon students, the more likely they are to at least try to evaluate more thoroughly. Contrary to what mass media outlets want us to believe, students are evaluating information. Is it thorough? No. Could it be better? Absolutely, and here is where I and the ACT UP method come in. It's placing the power in the hands of students so they can shine a light onto all the ways that information (mis)shapes our world views. We all exist in a world of influence and persuasion, and we owe it to everyone, including ourselves, to share reliable information to the best of our ability. Let's be honest. There will be missteps along the way, and we need to own our mistakes and commit to doing better next time. That's how accountability works.

The evaluation of information is the most important piece of information seeking. For years, librarians perfected research guides, instruction sessions, handouts, and tutorials around finding information whether it be online or through various databases. This is still important to teach but evaluating information must come first. The election in 2016 and the shitshow of a presidency thereafter proves this. Information is political. Information can be weaponized. Disinformation can cost lives. As librarians and educators, we need to make evaluating information our top priority because democracy depends on it. Using a method like ACT UP incorporates so much more than just who wrote the thing and when. ACT UP encourages students to think deeply and critically about how information is created, who has the privilege to do so, who gets to disseminate it, and what impact it has on the environment around them. Activism needs accurate information. We all deserve access to not only information but the ability to evaluate what we find.

What I am about to say is controversial, but I need to say it. We need to stop putting so much emphasis on citation styles and instead focus on evaluating sources. Seriously. I cannot tell you how many times I meet with students to help them navigate APA or MLA styles. I absolutely believe we need to cite our sources but when we put so much emphasis on a certain citation style, it takes time away from actually learning something that is far more useful. I promise that very few students leave college and go into the world citing sources in APA or MLA. There is a way to talk about citations that doesn't cause stress and anxiety and leaves room for much-needed conversations around evaluating information. What if we allowed students to create their own citation style? This allows students to really think about the pieces of information that are necessary to locate the resource. Librarian Kelly McElroy from Oregon State University did this in her instruction sessions and students were super creative in how they cited their sources, like incorporating emojis creative! When we make room for critical creativity, students make personal and meaningful connections to their assignments. The ACT UP evaluation method is a springboard for creative play.

For eight years I have taught with the ACT UP method along with other librarians across the globe. I know there is resistance from faculty and librarian colleagues. Some find the method too political, as if information and education are not political. Some folx live in states where teaching with the ACT UP method could cost them their jobs. Some folx don't think it is our place to talk about privilege in the classroom as that's too left leaning. I disagree. Information is my business. Information is what I do. When I am asked to come into the classroom to talk about 'library resources' I'm there to share my expertise. I bring it even if there are components that are hard to hear. Since that class in 2017, I have never asked for permission to talk about something specific during my library instruction and I am not about to start now. The sooner we put to rest the vocational awe around librarianship the sooner we can start dismantling the systemic oppression it firmly sits upon. For folx worried that students won't vibe well with this method, I say, 'Give it time.' For many students, the idea of privilege in publishing is a new concept. For marginalized students, it's a validation. For one-shot instruction sessions, there is not enough time to go in-depth on any one thing, so I just spend a few minutes showing them the method and dropping a little bit of knowledge about privilege to pique their interest.

But what about those of us who teach in red states where there are laws around talking about race, intersectionality, feminism and social justice in the classroom? Should we not bother? I think that would be a detriment to us all. I firmly believe there are ways to use the ACT UP evaluation method in a more covert way. Maybe some of the language is tweaked so that the word 'privilege' isn't spoken aloud. Maybe we emphasize some of the facets more than the others. Whatever we do, we must keep fighting for social justice. We have to keep showing up to help our disenfranchised students seize more power over their voices and stories.

ACT UP
EVALUATING SOURCES

LET'S EVALUATE SOURCES
PUSH AGAINST DOMINANT NARRATIVES
DISRUPT CITATION CIRCLES
BURST FILTER BUBBLES

AUTHOR
- Who wrote the resource?
- Google the authors - find out who they are
- Are they qualified to write about this topic?
- Do lateral reading
- Has the website or any of the authors been reported as a source of fake news?

CURRENCY
- What date was the resource published?
- Do you need to find current, up-to-date information?
- Does this resource's publication date meet the requirements of your assignment?
- If you are on a website, when was the last time it was updated?

TRUTH
- How accurate and reliable is this resource?
- Are there typos and spelling mistakes throughout the text?
- Can you verify any of the claims in other sources?
- Follow the rule of three - you should be able to back up claims in at least three of other sources.

UNBIASED
- There is no such thing as unbiased. We all have biases.
- We are looking for resources that are impartial.
- Who funded the research? Follow the money.
- Oftentimes funders have a vested interest in the research outcomes.

PRIVILEGE
- Privilege in publishing = mostly white male scholars and researchers.
- Ask yourself, are they the only folk that research and write about the topic?
- I mean, do only white males research and write about their findings? (HINT: NO!)
- Who is missing from the research conversation?

CREATED WITH CARE BY DAWN STAHURA

For more information, please visit:
https://www.dawnstahura.com/

The Work

Reflection Questions

- How do you incorporate evaluating sources into your classroom?
- Do you address privilege in terms of information creation and/or access?
- What evaluation methods do you currently use yourself and with your students?
- Could you see yourself incorporating the ACT UP evaluation method into your teaching?

Reflection Activities

- Use the ACT UP evaluation method to evaluate a new resource that you find. This can be something you stumble upon or something you choose that is outside your wheelhouse of expertise.
- Create your own citation style that addresses the essential elements.
- Assign your students to do the same.

Chapter 5

Air
Vision, Strategy, Intellect

Research is meaningful when it makes a difference to our communities.

We all have a scarcity mindset that prevents us from fully engaging with our work. Our inner critic takes over and informs us that we are not smart enough, talented enough, authentic enough, etc. to do whatever the thing is we want to accomplish. I have imposter syndrome. Even as I write this sentence, my inner critic, who I call Chad, is saying, 'You really have no idea what you are talking about.' *Thanks, Chad.* When I hear Chad, I am faced with two choices. I can either listen to Chad, close my laptop, and walk away feeling crappy about all the ways I am not enough, or I can practice mindfulness. By being mindful of the ways my intrapersonal rhetoric is impacting my mindset, I take my power back. Intrapersonal rhetoric is essentially our inner monologue (otherwise known as inner critics or imposter voices) that unconsciously affects the way we see ourselves and interact with our full potential. What I have learned by taking courses with Dr. Alexandria Peary is that through mindfulness practices we can learn to not only listen to our inner monologue but disrupt it and change it. Our intrapersonal rhetoric, inner critics and imposter syndromes are symptoms of scarcity mindset, and they prevent us from fully engaging with life. When I ask students what holds them back from doing research, most of them answer lack of confidence, time, and connection. The connection piece isn't just about vibing with their topics, it's how students feel inside the classroom. We cannot take in new information if we do not feel validated in the classroom. Why? Because we are too focused on our feelings of inadequacy, anxiety, and quite frankly, boredom.

Practicing mindfulness is the ability to hear our self-talk and/or Chad's ramblings and "train ourselves to first perceive the self-talk with non-evaluative detachment and then steer it through intention" (Peary, 2022, 4). Most of us exist in a state of mindlessness like when we drive to the grocery store but have no recollection of how we got there. Mindlessness is often described as being on autopilot. In Ellen Langer's (1989) book *Mindfulness* she discusses how our constant state of mindlessness has many different roots. I wholeheartedly believe that school is the taproot. Most of our schooling is focused on "goals rather than the process by which they are achieved. This single-minded pursuit of one outcome or another makes it difficult to have a mindful attitude about life" (Langer, p.34). We don't have to look very far to see this truth. Most students are fixated on grades and rubrics and it's no wonder. They have been brought up in the education system to value grades and rubrics. It's how students are taught to understand their value and worth. We spend very little time talking about the actual process of doing research and instead focus on the paper and all its necessary elements and attributes. No wonder most students dislike research when we frame it as a means to an end.

Another root of mindlessness is the belief that resources are limited, specifically intelligence (Langer, 1989, 27). Somewhere along the path from kindergarten to college, we are led to believe that only some folx can do *good research*. This scarcity mindset and/or deficit thinking, sets up students for failure. They already believe they cannot do it. It's more than just that they were never taught how to do research (or do it well) but the process of research was never modeled for them. There was never any transparency, only the finished published research papers. Of course, they believe they can't write research papers when all the papers they find are polished.

Let's imagine a 'typical' one-shot instruction session. We come into the classroom as students are getting situated. We spend a few minutes chatting with the faculty member (if the faculty member is even there), then the class starts, and we are introduced to do our 'thing'. Depending on what type of instruction we are giving, we may demo databases, show how to navigate the library catalog, talk about evaluating sources, and end it with questions. There may be questions but most often there is silence. We know that students are too embarrassed or afraid to ask for help, or they simply don't know what questions they have yet. They often don't know they have questions until they have questions. That's the nature of research and inquiry. We remind students how to contact us should they need any help after today and we leave. That was all done in 50 minutes (maybe less) which is not enough time to talk about the research process let alone build a sense of community which facilitates empathy in the room.

A guiding element of empathy is social justice work inside the classroom. Knowing that students arrive in a scarcity mindset helps us to navigate our responses and levels of engagement. A scarcity mindset convinces students that they lack essential resources to be successful. Again, these resources can be time, intellect, skills, experiences, money, etc. Our students are complete human beings who have lives and experiences outside the classroom that directly affect how they engage with the material we present to them. These unknown variables play a vital role in classroom dynamics, especially during a one-shot instruction session where precious little time is given to deliver content in a meaningful and impactful way. Over the years I have implemented certain small activities that yielded big results. I want to share these with you so that you can build a classroom based on social justice elements that leave students feeling not only seen but heard.

Building an inclusive community inside the classroom starts with proximities to power and shapes how students will interact with us. As educators, we are seen as people with authority and power over the students, regardless of how we see ourselves. Standing at the front of the classroom signals to students that we are important people, and our status is above them. So already, without doing anything, there is a power dynamic at play that influences the comfortability students feel towards us. We need to dismantle this power dynamic to build community while we are sharing space together.

The physical shape and layout of the class space directly impacts our capacity to learn. The standard way is by sitting in neat rows facing the person at the front of the room. Unless we are in a lab setting, rows create unnecessary silos between students. Rows establish a hierarchy which commands all eyes to the front. While students can, of course, turn their heads to hear their classmates speak, rows are not conducive to knowledge gathering and sharing. If students are to feel included, seen and heard then they must be able to see and hear each other. In contrast, a circle has no hierarchy, beginning, and end. Every person in the circle is just as important as the next. The power dynamic is evenly distributed, where everyone is seen and has a voice. Everyone can take ownership of the role they play as part of the circle. We, as the educators, become part of the circle and share space with the students. The proximity to power is disrupted which decreases student anxiety and disengagement. Being part of the circle is an honor, a gift and to be fully present in the circle we must show up as our authentic selves. This means as educators, we must share something of ourselves with the students. If we want students to be vulnerable, ask questions, try new things, and step outside of their comfort circles, we must model the behavior through active participation. Learning is an act of reciprocity. I recognize everyone's institution looks different as well as the actual classroom spaces we find ourselves teaching in. We might not be able to physically move chairs into a circle if we are in a big lecture hall or in a room where students are stacked on top of one another due to space issues on campus. Regardless of whether an actual circle shape can be made, at the very least a metaphorical circle can be created.

Research is a conversation: Building community in an instruction session.

I start with a two-minute drawing. I pass around a notecard to each student and ask them to crumple it up and then smooth it out the best they can. This small but powerful act helps students overcome the fear of the blank page. I set my phone timer for two minutes. Each student draws their portrait until the timer goes off. These portraits are meant to be a fun, icebreaker activity to ease us into our work for the day. I collect their portraits if I need to take attendance; otherwise, I ask them to put them aside until the end of class.

Depending on the classroom layout, we may move desks and/or chairs. Either way, we create a circle which serves two important purposes. First, it acts as a physical boundary setting whereby whatever or whoever is inside the circle is protected. Second, it provides a physical shift in the energy that alerts our senses that something new and/or different is occurring. Creating a circle prepares us for transformation. Starting the session with movement shifts the energy and equalizes us. We are all new to the circle.

Once we are settled, we engage in a naming ceremony where we all say our names, pronouns (if we feel comfortable doing so), and what our research and/or topic is. By stating our names, we are making connections to each other, witnessing each other's presence and voice. This does two things. First, naming has power, and we acknowledge that power by saying and hearing each other's names. Lerner and Fulambarker (2018) note, "respect and acceptance in the classroom often originate from something as simple as knowing someone's name" (p. 4). Second, research does not happen in isolation and oftentimes students come across research that does not fit their needs but might work for a classmate's project. I encourage researching in community with each other.

After introductions, I do a non-academic check-in. In the past I asked students how their research was going, what specific questions they had for me, and while I still ask those things during the session, I no longer start with them. The pandemic changed the way I create and hold space for students. I make space for how they are doing outside of academia so that our relationship-building is not tied solely to education. I want to know how they are as a person because I care about them as a person first. To build empathy, I must make space for the students to show up authentically which means bringing in experiences, thoughts, feelings, etc. that exist outside the classroom because it directly affects how they show up in the classroom. In physical and virtual spaces, I have used emotion prompts to facilitate these check-ins. Such as, *which Muppet are you today*, or *which Nicholas Cage are you feeling today*. These prompts get hilarious responses because they are so lighthearted and playful. Recently, I've started asking students *"what do you love about life?"* The shock and joy on their faces at being asked such a simple but powerful question builds a bridge that wasn't there before.

Next, I move into the research conversation. This is the heart of my instruction and I do some form of this in every session regardless of the topic and time constraints. Why? Because this is the chance for me to see where the students are and for them to learn from each other. Peer-to-peer learning cannot be underestimated, and the research conversation builds a community of practice over time. The questions I ask during the research conversation vary but they generally consist of asking students where they go for general information, where they go for academic information, how they evaluate the information they find, and how they know about current events. I am also curious how they interact with their topics daily. I am not surprised that most students answer Google (Scholar) to the first two questions. In fact, I am transparent that I also use Google (Scholar) dozens of times throughout the day to find information too. These questions allow students to see the similarities in their searching habits. I want students to have ownership over their research processes and skills. These questions disrupt the scarcity mindset because everyone has information-seeking skills. Everyone has some method to evaluate information and I want to acknowledge these skills, not devalue or diminish them. I want to add tools to their toolkit so they can find the right resources for their informational needs, knowing that those needs constantly change and evolve.

I am always surprised by the answers I get when students discuss how they evaluate. Many students are googling authors, looking up citations at the end of articles, doing lateral reading (even if they don't call it this) and practicing what I call *the rule of three,* where they search to see if they can find the claims supported in at least three other sources. I have never been in a classroom where students admitted they do not evaluate at all. Not once. Depending on the student responses, I ask probing questions like, *"why would it matter if a researcher sits on a specific association, organization or company? Why is it important to follow the money and see who funds the research? Why would it matter to pay attention to who the authors cite in their research?"* These questions open the door for conversations on bias, privilege in publishing and shoddy research. I've had colleagues accuse me of opening Pandora's Box. After all, students should choose academic resources over stuff they find doing a rudimentary Google search. If we view the research process as simplistic (which it is not), then sure, push academic articles and call it a day. I believe that would be cheating our students. Academic articles are important, I'm not arguing that, but I am pushing back against the notion that academic resources are the only valid forms of scholarship. I am real with students when I say that the general population does not read academic articles to learn about current events. When I ask, *"do you think your friends, family, and/or neighbors are at home right now chilling, reading a scholarly article?",* the students laugh and say no because even if they don't have specific reasons for why their neighbors aren't reading academic journals, they understand there is a very real information divide. There are many reasons for this divide such as lack of access due to financial cost, lack of understanding academic jargon, lack of easy access to public libraries, etc. So, when I follow up with, *"then how do they know about x, y, and z?"* The answer is obvious, mainstream media.

The liveliest conversations happen when we discuss mainstream media. Students talk about the gap between what is known in academia and what is highlighted in news segments. These are important conversations because they illustrate why paying attention to where you get your information, who the authors are, and what the motivation is behind the resource, are so important. It's more than just collecting articles to complete a research assignment. It's about being fully invested in the overall research process.

It's acknowledging that researching has an emotional price tag. We don't ask students how emotions play a role in their research. Maybe we don't think they do or maybe we don't want to talk about emotions because we believe that emotions have no place inside the classroom (or the academy for that matter). To practice empathy is to investigate the emotional side of research. Absolutely our emotions play a pivotal role in how we interact with information so why should research be any different? When I ask, *"do you think your emotions play a role in how you interact, select, and use information?"*, they all nod their heads yes. In every class session, there are students relieved that this question was asked because they feared they were the only ones whose emotions got in the way of research. Remember the scarcity mindset? Well, here it is again. Our emotions are a critical piece of the research process, yet we never talk about them. If we are to engage with our students holistically then we must talk about the emotional side of research. If we want to build an inclusive community where students are seen and heard, we must work with the emotional side of information seeking. Achieving empathy depends on it.

Beyond a head nod, students talk about how they don't feel smart enough to do the research because they don't understand the jargon. Others mention that they only want to find resources that fit their viewpoints even though they know it's problematic. Some say that by purposefully seeking out differing viewpoints, they are bombarded with information that is hurtful and sometimes hateful. Others say that after searching for a million years, they just take whatever they can find because they are tired and overwhelmed with the entire process. All these responses are valid and truthfully, all things I have experienced myself. This transparency is where empathy comes in. I remind students that our minds need rest just as our bodies do. Research fatigue is real and affects us all. We don't have to find all your sources in one sitting. In fact, we won't so it's best to not set ourselves up for failure. Research is a process that takes time and so we need ample time to fully engage.

We must be kind to ourselves as we are (un)learning. Purposely seeking out contradictory information is challenging so we need to be mindful of the potential impact that information can have on us mentally and emotionally. Seeking out alternative viewpoints can be a beautiful disruption, but we need to be prepared for the storm as well. Asking for help makes this process easier! No one has to go through the research process alone. I encourage students to find an accountability buddy to work on projects together. There is power in showing up for yourself and for your community. I remind students that I am here to help and that by asking for help they recognize the value in themselves and their work. This value piece, once understood, stays with them beyond the classroom.

By now you may be wondering how long the research conversation lasted. On average it takes around 10-15 minutes although the time can be adjusted depending on time restraints. Even a quick 5-minute conversation is better than nothing. Once this is wrapped up, we move into my demonstration of the 'the thing' and engage in active learning. It's time to shift the energy in the room, so this may mean putting the room back into its original layout or having students stand up and stretch. Taking a quick break awakens our senses and grounds us in the receiving of new information.

Active learning should be creative play. It is a chance to apply what they have just learned. After a quick check-in to see how we are feeling, it's time to play. This could look like think/pair/share, reflection writing and/or one of the activities I discuss in this chapter. The point of active learning is to make connections between information and action. Once the session comes to a close, I state the three most important takeaways. Every one of my sessions has the same three takeaways. The first is that the research guide, the library resources, (whatever I showed them) exists and they can come back to it when they are ready. The second is that I exist as a person in the world and I'm there to help them. The third is the most important. I ask students to take out the portrait they drew at the beginning of class, turn it over to the blank side and write, *I matter. Always.* I can tell you that this really affects folx. Students have told me they put it on their bathroom mirror, hung it above their desk, and carried it around with them as a reminder of how important they are in the world. This small act that literally takes a second has the biggest impact with lasting effects This, my friends, is how we build empathy despite time constraints.

I know these activities can be challenging and push us outside our own comfort circles, but our students need this. Maybe you won't get to cover one or two things because you made time for conversation. Okay, cool. Now ask yourself what the real takeaway from your sessions is. What do you want the students to know? Is it how to use specific resources? I believe that engaging in thoughtful conversations around research is far more important and meaningful. Our goal should be connecting students to information-seeking techniques that are applicable to all facets of their lives. To do this, we might have to give something up.

But what if you teach online? From March 2020 to September 2021 all my instruction sessions were via Zoom. Obviously, students could not form a physical circle in a virtual space, so we created them metaphorically. We all know what a good Zoom meeting looks and feels like. We also know how challenging creating a community can be for virtual spaces. Over the summer 2020 I enrolled in a workshop led by Nikki Pelonia, who was the best Zoom facilitator I've ever had. Part of his success is his genuine enthusiasm and empathy to create inclusive spaces but the other is the activities he used, in particular *pass the popcorn*. Nikki would start by introducing himself, his pronouns and how he was feeling that day based on a scale of 1-10. Then he would *pass the popcorn* to someone else in the call. This person would do their introductions and *pass the popcorn* to someone else. As the facilitator, Nikki would keep track of who introduced themselves, so no one was left out and to help folx *pass the popcorn* if they were not sure who to pass it to. This activity is successful because it holds each person accountable for not only introducing themselves but inviting the next person to do the same. Because we didn't know when we would be called, we had to pay attention and possibly even take notes on who had spoken. This activity is not just for introductions. We can apply it anytime we need group involvement. For students who cannot turn on their mics or camera, the chat feature is a fine alternative.

Breakout rooms are another way to create community in virtual spaces. Before sending students into their rooms, we can invite them to work together to create discussion norms. These are critical in making sure everyone understands how to interact with each other and the material inside the space. Once inside the breakout rooms, we can ask students to share their naming stories. This is simply telling others where our names came from. Sharing our naming stories builds connection and a way to see and hear each other. There is power in naming. Giving students the opportunity to share their naming stories gives their presence power in the room. I've used this technique dozens of times and I am always amazed at how quickly connections between students are made. Someone's story always resonates and when it does, it takes away some of the anxiety and fear. Another activity we can do is randomly put students into breakout rooms and tell them they are in that specific group because they all have something in common. By way of conversation, they will discover what those commonalities are. I've never had a group report back that they had nothing in common because with dedicated time and space, we discover how we are alike.

Social justice in the classroom is leveraging my privilege to lift others, decenter whiteness, hierarchy, and power to make space for student knowledge and experiences which facilitate inclusive research conversations. Intentionality sits at the core of my social justice work. By centering intention, I can humanize research and the creative process. WHY we do something is just as important as HOW we do it. I'm often invited into classes to teach something specific like zines, the ACT UP evaluation method, oppressive classification systems and semantics, and fighting back against fake news. What these specific sessions have in common is their role in social justice work. I've developed the following activities to strengthen the connection between ourselves and the role we each have in dismantling systems of oppression.

Air Activities

Naming Stories

We all have a story behind our names but rarely are we given space and the opportunity to share it. To teach holistically, we need to know each other's names despite how long our time together will be because despite the length of time, the power of the naming story will stay with us. We build community through storytelling. It's how we remember. This activity works best if students are sitting in a circle so that everyone can see and hear each other. I usually go first to not only model what I am asking but to quell any nervousness that students might be feeling in the room. Naming stories can be as simple as "my mother named me Dawn because she liked the name. I never really liked my name but over time it kinda grew on me." Some students will share ancestral stories, a deep love or dislike of their names, and what they wished their names were. I've had some students talk about their deadnames without ever having to speak them. Naming stories also help us remember each other's name. It's easier to remember "Stevie who is named after Stevie Nicks" than just the name Stevie with nothing tied to it.

Mantra of Intention

We all have an inner critic, and we almost never talk openly about it. We certainly never talk about what it says to us and how it prevents us from doing the work we need/want to do. My son, Rowan, just turned 5-years-old and his inner critic has not found him yet. It is a beautiful and liberating thing to watch Rowan create without fear of judgment, embarrassment, or that he lacks the talent or skills to do it. He has that beginner's mind that allows him to create without reservations. Inner critics tend to find their voices around that time in childhood when we realize we and our creations are being judged. At some point as children, we realized that there was a 'right' way to do things. To do things 'successfully' we needed a certain level of talent and skill to be taken seriously. For some of us this is where we stopped being creative. We put down our art supplies, microphones, dance shoes, etc. and traded them in for other more 'practical' and 'sensible' things. We moved through adolescence and into adulthood telling ourselves we were uncreative, untalented, and certainly not an artist of any kind. We just weren't *creative in THAT way* whatever THAT way may be for us. Most of us never considered the fact that all of this could be a lie. Yet that is exactly what it is, a lie. I've worked with folx aged four all the way to 87, and I can tell you with absolute certainty that everyone is creative. Everyone has a story to tell, and every single life has meaning and significance. Sure, not everyone has the level of artist talent that Frida Kahlo had or the writing ability of Joy Harjo yet that doesn't mean that creativity is beyond our grasp. Quite the contrary.

Creativity is our inherent birthright. We all have the ability to create, and we should create. I define creativity as our inherent birthright to imagine different and plausible worlds. Talent, on the other hand, takes time, practice, and perseverance. Established creators know this but rarely do they talk about it which creates this mysticism around creativity.

The research process is messy (as it should be). There is no 'one right way' to engage with it. Once students realize this, they can create the space to research, write and then later, revise in whatever way feels right. If they can step away from all the rules (and overly formalized styles of writing) and just be in the process, they can learn to let go of the idealized final product and enjoy a beginner's mindset.

The world needs creativity. The world needs art in whatever form it takes from folx just like us. Of course, the world needs the heroic feats of those trailblazers who pave the way for others, who tear down the status quo and fight against the system but for most of us, we will do our fighting at the micro level. Sometimes that is more impactful than the big grand-sweeping gestures, especially for the communities we are a part of. Creativity is more than just painting, writing, and playing music. It can be something "less tangible such as a scientific theory, an idea of urban renewal, or a new way of teaching, mentoring, parenting, leading, collaborating, meditating, or serving those in need" (Astin, 2004, p. 4). When articulated this way, it is easier to see just how creative we all are and can be.

We live in a microcosm. Everything we do has a rippling effect. Just by being in the world, we make a difference and without us, the microcosm we are a part of would drastically change. In full transparency, I speak from experience here. I lost my 17-year-old niece, Elise, to suicide and I cannot put into the words the rippling affect her death had on others. The truth is, we will never know the impact our life has on others, but trust me when I say that our absence would be felt. So, when our inner critics pop up to tell us that we can't or shouldn't do a thing, we must find ways to silence that voice so that we can do the work that calls us. The work that we need to put out into the world. The work that matters and is life changing even if the only life changed is our own. My inner critic likes to tell me that I suck at writing. That it is a waste of time for me to be writing this book because no one will read it and if they do read it, they will hate it. My inner critic assures me that I will receive bad reviews for this book. Maybe some of this is true but I won't know unless I actually write this book and put it out into the world. The purpose of our inner critic is to protect us, to stop us from potentially getting hurt, but we can't foster empathy, community, and connection without putting ourselves and our work out there. We have to risk stepping outside our comfort circles.

I fight against my inner critic by first humanizing it. Naming it allows me to call it out and question it. I call my inner critic Chad. I am sorry if this is offensive to folx who are named Chad, have friends, or loved ones named Chad but for me, I have never met a Chad I liked. I encourage you to name your inner critic so that the next time it starts mouthing off, you can say something like, *I hear you Chad but what evidence do you have that this will suck?* Here's the thing. Chad doesn't have any evidence. He is fueled by fear, intra- and interpersonal rhetoric, and a craving for repetitiveness, because we feel safe when we do things we already know how to do.

The most effective method I've found for silencing Chad is to create a mantra of intention. As Alexandria Peary (2022) writes in *Mantra of Intention*, creating a mantra "puts us in the spiritual and creative state of mindfulness for the sake of our writing and ourselves as writers" (p. 3). I find creating mantras of intention work just as effectively when engaged with the research process. The purpose of the mantra is to become aware of the negative self-talk (i.e. Chad) and disrupt that narrative with positive, self-compassion. Mantras repeated over time become a healing truth that allows us to overcome roadblocks and missteps. By setting our intention, we redirect the power from our mindlessness state (i.e. Chad) into a mindfulness state. When students begin the research process by creating a mantra of intention, they are creating space to be more mindful. Whenever they feel that they are sinking under the weight of confusion, negative self-talk, or fear, they can come back to their mantra of intention to regroup and ground themselves. If I see students struggling with finding sources or understanding certain concepts, I stop the session and provide space for the students to create a mantra of intention. Right then and there. Here are a few mantras of intention I have created.

I am. I am. I am.
All the power you need is already inside of you.

Drawing Occupations

During my time at Simmons University, I was blessed with the opportunity to teach a course called "Mending Paths for Social Change." The course focused on information spectrums, zines, and personal narrative writing as a form of scholarly writing and research. This is by far the most impactful and inspiring course I've ever designed and taught. The course itself used zines and personal narrative writing as the lens to look at information spectrums. The course blended research, writing, and various forms of critical creativity. The first time I taught the course I had eight students, and they were hungry to do something different. There were no exams in my course or research papers. Instead, we answered daily journal prompts, had weekly student-led discussions, and researched a community we were a part of which culminated into a personal zine (perzine) as their final projects. Each student presented their zine on the last day of class. Despite the nervousness some students felt, the community we built during the semester was one of support and empathy. In the Fire chapter I will share some of the exercises we did as a class but for now I want to talk about a simple art activity that changed the way I now present the concept of bias in the classroom.

I love Lynda Barry. I had just finished reading her book, *Syllabus: Notes from an Accidental Professor,* (which I highly recommend) and wanted to try the simple exercise of drawing occupations with my students. Originally, I brought the activity into the classroom as a warm-up before we dove into our student-led discussions. The activity involves using simple shapes (circles, squiggles, squares, etc.) to draw character occupations. The main goal is to draw enough information including props and/or accessories so that the character's occupation is immediately identifiable. For example, I might draw a librarian wearing glasses and holding a stack of books. I decided to not have occupations preselected and instead let each student name an occupation. They named occupations before they knew what the activity was. Some of the occupations were an occupational therapist, a dentist, a grocery clerk, and a neuroscientist. Once each person wrote their occupation on the whiteboard, I told them the specifics of the activity. We would have five minutes to draw each of the occupations based on Lynda Barry's guidelines of simple shapes. I limited the activity to five minutes because I didn't want my students to overthink it. Because I never ask students to do something I haven't done, I added an occupation (psychic) to the list and drew along with them. In fact, I always did the activities with the students not just because they were fun but because I wanted to know firsthand how the activities felt.

Once the five minutes were up, we shared our drawings. Now here is where something interesting happened, that unexpected thing that so often happens when true deep learning is occurring. We noticed collectively the biases inherent in our drawings. Why was the dentist depicted as male in all our drawings? Why was no one drawn with a visible disability? How come the psychic was drawn with stereotypical accessories that likened that image to racist depictions of Romani people? This sparked an intense and critical conversation around inherent biases and how each of us were affected by them. That simple yet powerful exercise has been incorporated in so many of my instruction sessions since, to talk and literally illustrate what unconscious bias is. What starts out as a fun ice breaker activity ends up being an eye-opening experience of bias. For the sake of time, I now select the occupations for the students to draw. Usually the occupations are chemist, doctor, librarian, and cyclist simply because I know what biases and stereotypes will be depicted. These biases are deeply ingrained in our collective psyche and what better way to talk about them than through the lens of art and creativity. I now use this activity when I am presenting at conferences, both in-person and virtually as a warm-up activity. I don't tell the participants the real purpose of the activity until the end of the presentation.

Who Am I and What Do I Bring—Identity Mapping

All of us are made up of numerous identities that intersect. We all have identities that provide us privilege and others that land on the side of the oppressed. Understanding how our identities intersect is critical to dismantling systemic oppression inside and outside the classroom. Building community and teaching from a place of empathy requires that we acknowledge our intersecting identities and teach to the whole person, not just one aspect of who our students are. So often students are scared and/or intimidated to share their identities and for good reason. For others, they might not have given much thought to how their identities interact and intersect. One activity I use is the *who am I and what do I bring* worksheet. This worksheet is modeled after and adapted from the work done by Jamie Washington from the Social Justice Training Institute and Rebecca Latin from the Southern Poverty Law Center as well as anti-bias workshops led by Stacy Collins, Shari Johnson, and Lisa Smith-McQueenie. Before we can understand the positions, we take on topics we need to know who we are and how that shapes the way we move in the world. This seems simple, but the truth is, a lot of students, especially those who are more privileged, have never sat and thought about their identities, so they struggle with this activity. Intersectionality is critical in social justice movements and for bringing social justice frameworks into the classroom. By understanding who we are, we can begin the work of seeing others and learning to move past stereotypes and racist tropes. This exercise illustrates just how complex and complicated we are and how binaries are part of White supremacy culture. Gray areas exist and for many of us, we live inside those gray areas with multiple intersecting identities.

Obviously, this worksheet cannot be administered during a one-shot instruction session, but it can be incorporated in a flipped classroom model whereby students complete the worksheet before the instruction session. For folx who teach semester or quarter long classes, workshops, and/or seminars, this worksheet could be the start of a much broader and more critical conversation around identities and systems of oppression. I've taught with this worksheet in a variety of disciplines such as healthcare studies, biology, social sciences, and the humanities, both in-person and virtually. You might be wondering how this worksheet ties into instruction. This activity gives students the space to think about who they are and how this might affect the way they interact with information. Who we are and how we feel about our identities and the world around us has a significant impact on the types of information we seek, how we evaluate it and how we use it. The worksheet reveals the student's intersectionality and how and why they are drawn to specific information sources and strategies. Connecting these two concepts is not an immediate leap but one that must be critically dissected and discussed. This is where class conversations, small groups, and even think/pair/shares can provide powerful opportunities for (un)learning. For example, I've taught sessions where one of the main themes was on semantics and how oppressive knowledge systems prevent students from seeing themselves accurately represented inside those systems. This activity was used as the starting off point to a larger class conversation on how semantics matter. Once identities are mapped out, how we search for information, how information is organized and classified, and what we do with the information we find becomes powerful tools in dismantling oppressive systems inside and outside the classroom.

My template is just that, a template. I encourage folx to adapt it to fit their own communities and classrooms. You know your environment so ask the questions that need to be asked and start difficult conversations from a place of identity mapping. One suggestion I have for engaging students in difficult conversations is to provide a non-directed art making activity to do while students discuss their worksheets. This art making activity can be as simple as doodling and/or coloring. According to research compiled by Concordia University's Art Hives Network (2018), engaging in non-directed artmaking "helped expression and containment of arising emotions, thoughts, or visions that might have been more difficult to express verbally" (p.5). You'll need to bring some art supplies such as crayons, colored pencils, coloring sheets, and blank paper.

Positionality Statements

A step beyond the *who am I and what do I bring* worksheet are positionality statements. These take more time and are more nuanced than filling out a worksheet. I've worked on positionality statements with students, colleagues, and friends so they are not confined to academia. Every aspect of our lives is impacted by our positionalities. Our positions on what is important to us and how our values shape our movement in the world are critical to building community, participating in active listening, and constructively engaging with folx who might not share our same ideologies. Sometimes we might not know where we stand on an issue until we sit down and think critically about it. For a lot of us, our privilege shields us from seeing and experiencing systemic oppression. White supremacy is so pervasive because it tries to be invisible. Positionality statements are one way to create visibility.

Another purpose of writing positionality statements is to see where you are an expert and where you are a novice. While some folx might disagree with me, I believe that we are all experts of something even if that *something* is our own lived experiences. The reason to write positionality statements is to map out what you are (un)learning as a person. When we consider our experiences and expertise, we can identify what areas we need to invest more energy into (un)learning, such as biases that came to light, and misinformation or harmful stereotypes we played into at one time. The more information we have about our positions the better we are at navigating unknown terrain with empathy and understanding.

There are numerous ways to write a positionality statement and a simple Google search will yield you tons of templates to start with. You can find positionality statements from the lens of a researcher, educator, student, etc. I created a worksheet that I use to get students started on the brainstorming that goes into positionality statements. The worksheet is inspired and informed by the work done by Dez Alaniz, Archivist at the Presidio Research Center of Santa Barbara and the *wheel of power/privilege* image by Sylvia Duckworth. You can use both the *who am I and what do I bring* worksheet and the *positionality statement* worksheet together as they complement each other well or get creative and design your own. The most important part is doing the work, not the worksheet design we use. Positionality statements are not 'one and done' but something we revisit frequently as we continue to (un)learn. I encourage folx to write one a year as an accountability piece, a self check-in to see where we are now, to recognize how far we have come and what (un)learning still needs to happen. I want to reiterate that positionality statements are not just for academics although they are commonly situated there to talk about our approach to teaching and research. Positionality statements can and should be used in community activism, co-ops, schools of all kinds (elementary, secondary, etc.), workshop facilitations, writing groups, and anywhere else where inherent biases prevent folx from authentically interacting with information and others. So, basically any place where humans are alive and thinking.

Empathetic Peer Review

> "I am open to critique, of course, if they are offered in the spirit of collective liberation."
>
> adrienne marie brown

Ah, the mysterious process of peer review that leaves students riddled with anxiety. Peer review is touted as the gold standard for scholarship. Most students understand to some extent what peer review is and why we do it. Before I say what I am about to say, I want to make clear that I am a fan of peer review. It has its place in academia and absolutely prevents some potentially harmful research from making its way into publication. Just like academia itself, peer review is built upon systemic oppression. The truth is not everyone is able to publish their research simply because they do not have the same publishing privilege as their white colleagues. When we ask students to locate peer reviewed articles for their research, this privilege piece is never really talked about. Most students are happy to find any scholarly article that fits the rubric requirements for the assignment. It's the lack of investigating privilege that causes citation circles to form where only the same white folx get cited, effectively leaving out research that is just as good if not better. We must teach our students how to critically evaluate articles through the lens of privilege. Looking critically at peer review isn't just about who gets to publish but also being transparent that just because something is peer reviewed does not make it infallible. It's a disservice to not tell our students the truth because NOTHING created by humans is ever without bias, flaws, and under the influence of systematic oppression. There is shoddy research out there. In our databases. Calling out shoddy research is the whole reason why the website Retraction Watch exists. While honest mistakes happen, some research is knowingly and deliberately falsified, oftentimes around money and prestige. Corporations, especially pharmaceutical companies, pay out big money for research to put a delightful spin on known lethal side effects. Teaching students how to follow the money is a crucial piece of understanding privilege in peer review. Let's not forget about peer review rings where folx band together to peer review each other's work. Big publishing giants like Sage have discovered peer review and citation rings within their publications. Our students need to be aware of this. Evaluation of resources cannot and should not stop just because something is found in a peer reviewed journal. We need to remain critical of any type of resource that comes our way.

Even though peer review has a dark side (I mean, what doesn't), it does work, and we absolutely should be providing students with the experience of peer review inside the classroom. What better way for students to understand what the process is than by going through something similar with their classmates. Implementing peer review in the classroom, in workshops, and other spaces where students are creating is a great way to elicit feedback and constructive criticism. Truth be told, we all need to get more comfortable hearing and giving constructive criticism because if we and our egos cannot handle getting it from our peers, we certainly cannot handle it from folx outside our circles. I've seen a few writers and artists over the years stop creating simply because of negative feedback from the public. If we are to be agents of change, lead with empathy and show up authentically, we have to put ourselves out there for criticism. We will get criticized. I'm being criticized right now. I guarantee it.

Implementing an empathetic peer review process is about accountability. It's showing up and doing the work and allowing that work to be evaluated by a peer. It's reciprocity and it's a skill needed in the world. Empathetic peer review is a form of spiritually witnessing. If we understand peer review on a micro level, we can understand it on a macro. I mean, sure, they are not *really* the same and they are really the same. One place I have seen the importance and power of peer review is around creating zines in the classroom.

Several years ago, I worked with a sociology professor who assigned zines as a final project. The class was divided up into groups and each group decided what topic to research under the umbrella of inequality. Each group researched, wrote, and published their zines. On the last day of class, each group went around the room and sat with each group's zine and peer reviewed it. The peer review process itself, including what questions to ask and how many points were assigned to each question, was determined by class consensus earlier in the semester. Watching the students critically and empathetically review each other's zine was remarkable. Each group articulated what worked, what needed more research, and what points of confusion they were left with. Each group critiqued both the written content and the use of images. Were the images just taking up space or were they telling their own story? Were the images illustrating the main points of the zine? Did the written content and the images complement each other in the overall aesthetic of the zine? This style of empathetic peer review and gallery walk combination allowed for movement and energy in the room. Each group had a certain amount of time with each zine before they had to get up and move to the next zine. At the end of the class, the peer review sheets were given to the professor and counted towards a percentage of their final grade. What the students had to say mattered! It wasn't some mindless activity that was assigned but rather an important piece of the research process. It not only demystified the peer review process but allowed students to use their voices and the knowledge they gained throughout the semester.

The type of peer review I just described is certainly more empathetic and compassionate than the academic peer review process in scholarship. I am more than okay with this. First off, our students should gain experience in peer review by way of empathy and solidarity. Some may argue that this just sets the students up for disappointment later or that we are providing coddling/handholding when the real world doesn't. I believe that if we teach our students to critically evaluate their peer's work through an empathetic lens, it opens the doorway for others to do the same. Micro to macro. Also, this type of empathetic peer review allows students the opportunity to provide additional information or points of consideration for their peer reviewers. These points of consideration are not weaknesses but places in the research where there were stumbles, pitfalls, and/or facepalms. One of the best aspects of empathetic peer review is the ability to articulate what was experienced by engaging with the piece. What did I feel, see, and/or imagine? How could what I read impact me and the world around me? The more vulnerable we are the more honest a review. The most informative peer review is the one that successfully articulates a shift, that experience, or feeling that was elicited from interacting with the work.

Empathetic peer review is not limited to just a written critique or assessment. What if we broadened the idea of what thoughtful and constructive criticism could look like? What if students responded to their peers with a drawing, or a poem, meme, or doodle? What if we allowed for greater creativity and imagination when it came to the peer review process? One could argue that being able to respond to research/art/etc. in more than one way helps both the reviewer and reviewee. This multimodal peer review is often done in expressive art therapy whereby someone creates a piece, and someone responds to it in a different modality. We have a lot to learn from the arts and if we adopt some of these techniques into our instruction sessions, we will teach holistically and with more empathy. What matters is the quality of the review, not the medium by which it was presented. Allowing students to choose which form of empathetic peer review most resonates gives them more control over their (un)learning.

Empathetic peer review can happen inside and outside the classroom. In fact, it can happen outside of academia! Maybe you are part of a writing circle, an art group, or a business co-op. The places and situations where empathetic peer review can happen are endless. Anywhere that creative work exists there is a place for peer review. You just have to be open to it. Participating in the peer review process not only helps you articulate the information you learn but improves your ability to convey that articulation in a thoughtful and meaningful way that is not based on judgment or hostility. Empathetic peer review comes from a place of building community and lifting each other up without being condescending or sugarcoating our criticisms. It's about being accountable for our own work and the work we do for others. It's about deep listening, sitting with our insecurities and opening ourselves up to opportunities to learn more about ourselves and others. Expressive Arts Therapist, Shaun McNiff (1998) posits in his book *Trust the Process: An Artist's Guide to Letting Go*, that the best peer reviews happen in places where students feel safe, and they know that there is going to be ongoing support during the process. He reminds us that criticism is harder to hear once the project is finished. Students are more receptive to feedback during the formative process. Which makes sense. The question, *"what would you like me to do about it* now?" becomes the statement *"I'm glad you pointed this out before I turned it in for a grade."*

So, what types of things can be peer reviewed? Well, anything. I've led instruction sessions where students paired and peer reviewed research questions, thesis statements, keywords, and search plans. Another set of eyes is always better than one and each person learns something new. Any part of the research process can be peer reviewed and it is an effective way to get students comfortable with research, especially if they have not done it before. Having a peer look over their work from formulating a research question all the way to the first draft is beneficial to everyone because we all need support. As Shaun McNiff (1998) suggests in *Trust the Process: An Artist's Guide to Letting Go*, criticism is much harder to hear once a thing is finished so by implementing peer review alongside the research process, students do not feel so 'attacked' by criticisms. Peer review is an activity that can happen outside the classroom if there is not enough time to devote to it during class time. We can assign students to read each other's research plan and review it. Having a template at the ready is helpful for guiding students through the peer review process. Art such as paintings, drawings, sculptures, etc. can be peer reviewed as well as artists' statements. Creative writing and writing in general are also excellent for a peer review. Community guidelines, lesson plans, positionality statements, strategic plans, vision statements, as well as business plans can all benefit from it as well. We need to be open to the idea and apply it to whatever our students are working on. Is there a way to get constructive criticism and feedback that comes from a place of empathy? Would this thing our students are creating benefit from empathetic peer review? Chances are it absolutely would, and they will benefit too.

Accountability Sessions

Pairing nicely with peer review are accountability sessions. This is where students show up and do a thing independently together. The point is to hold each other and themselves accountable for the work. This could look like writing sessions, research sessions, or working on creative projects. Many students feel guilty for carving out time for themselves, especially if it involves something creative. Capitalism tells them that their work is not valuable or important unless it is generating a profit. (The profit is not for them but for capitalism itself).

Creative works are usually not deemed valuable by capitalism unless they can be marketed and sold to the masses for millions of dollars. No one I know is making millions of dollars; nonetheless, creativity is important and quite frankly, priceless. Our students' work is valuable whether the establishment and the status quo agree or not. Since students feel guilty working on creative projects independently, holding themselves accountable to do the work is hard. They often don't set aside time to create or if they do, they feel bad about it. They cannot create something beautiful and meaningful with a scarcity mindset. Holding accountability sessions is one way to bring students together to work on their projects without judgment or guilt. Sessions can be in physical or virtual spaces. I attended weekly accountability sessions with other writers while I wrote this book. There is something powerful about sharing space with a community of others working on something that is important to us. The session I attended was via Zoom. There was no music, and everyone was muted. Folx just wrote. I collapsed the Zoom screen so that I could periodically see someone else writing, but for the most part I was doing my thing while others were doing theirs. At the hour mark, we said our goodbyes and left. It was an hour where I was accountable to myself and my writing group. I spiritually witnessed their presence as they witnessed mine. It was powerful and effective. I got so much writing done in that hour that I otherwise wouldn't have. Why? Because without the accountability piece, I was more prone to distractions. You know, checking emails, looking at various social media platforms, or watching a YouTube video or two. I did not feel guilty about spending time working on my book. Our students deserve the time and space to create. Accountability sessions provide them with that.

Depending on the needs of the accountability session, students can establish goals that help them stay on track. They get to decide what happens during their accountability sessions. Coming to a consensus will foster a community of practice where they all get their needs met. If students feel accomplished, they continue to show up and be accountable. Imagine what they could create if given the space and time to do so!? The classroom is the perfect place to find accountability buddies. Students don't have to be working on the same project to participate. In fact, having different projects and topics creates communities of practice where students can learn about ideas and subjects that they might not have ever thought about before. It opens the possibility of future partnerships and research ideas that might span across disciplines. Aside from this, students in accountability sessions will, of course, talk. This closed environment is perfect for venting, finding common ground, and discovering similarities. It's a modern version of consciousness raising. Most students I work with do not have a sense of belonging on campus or in academia. Being in a space where peer to peer conversations happen allows for a sense of community to form. Belonging is born from community. And what better space for accountability sessions to happen than inside the library. At my institution's library we have a makerspace where students can drop by and work on projects, oftentimes sitting with students from other courses. For those of us at institutions that devalue the worth of the library, our spaces that facilitate accountability sessions is one way we can show the connection between student belonging and retention. Students who feel like they belong, stay.

The Work

Reflection Questions

- What areas in your life are you an expert?
- Where in your life might an accountability session be useful?
- What is your naming story?
- Have you ever thought about mindless versus mindfulness states of being?

Reflection Activities

- Name your inner critic and then create a mantra of intention.
- Complete either who *am I and what do I bring* or the *positionality statement* worksheet and see what you learn about yourself.
- Do the *occupational drawings* with someone and compare your results. Reflect on the biases and stereotypes that are present.

Chapter 6

Water
Spirituality, Healing

Our entire living is a spiritual practice.
  Tricia Hersey

This is the chapter I struggled with the most because I know folx have strong feelings around spirituality. I invite you to step outside your comfort circle with the intention of seeing the world through a spiritual lens. I'm not here to recruit you into the realm of spirituality. Even if that were a thing (it isn't), I'm not one to get all up in someone else's beliefs. I want to share what spirituality means to me and how I incorporate it into the classroom.

I want to discuss two laws of spirituality. The first is the law of attraction otherwise known as *like attracts like.* Basically, this means that whatever we put out into the world, we receive back. We can and do influence the space around us. Just think about a time you were in a bad mood. Imagine a room where students are ready to learn and you enter radiating negativity. That negativity, that energy emitting from you, would affect the students. In fact, their moods would change solely by the energy shift you created by entering the room. What this law beautifully illustrates is that we have the power to influence the environment around us. If we engage with others from a place of empathy, they will respond to us in kind.

The second is the law of contagion. Whatever we encounter continues to be influenced by us long after we leave. While this sounds a little hocus pocus, think about teaching. We provide students with the information and skills to understand difficult and sometimes complex subject matter. Those students go on to use that information and skillsets in other instances outside the classroom. They may or may not remember we taught them this information, but they are definitely still influenced by us. This is the law of contagion. We all have and will influence others by the decisions we make, the art we create, and the spaces we cultivate. There is immense power in the law of contagion and folx committed to social justice are cognizant of this and the ways in which it builds and shapes community. Another useful way to think about this concept is through the ripple effect. I've seen this firsthand with the zines that my students have created. Their stories go on to live outside the classroom in physical and digital form. Who encounters their zine once it leaves their hands is unknown and the impact continues to ripple out. The same is true for educating with empathy. What we share with students will go on to affect not only them, but everyone else they encounter.

I start with these two laws to show that seemingly "spiritual" things happen around us and to us every day. It's a matter of context and how we frame our experiences. Most of us are spiritual beings, and yet we are conditioned to dismember that part of ourselves when we walk into a classroom. But we do not live in an "either/or" world despite what we have been told. The world is an "AND" place where we get to be multi-faceted and fluid. "AND movements" recognize that two things can be true at the same time without lessening the importance or impact of both things. I am spiritual AND a librarian. I am constantly learning AND I am an expert. 'AND movements' are an essential component to dismantling patriarchal systems and White supremacy. White supremacy loves to establish either/or situations because they strip away the complexity of the items being either/ored (Okun & Jones, 2000). Based on either/or thinking, I am either spiritual or a librarian. I cannot be both. Issues are either black or white, good or bad, right or wrong. This type of thinking creates unnecessary urgency and conflict as it does not consider the intersectionality of identities nor the complexities of moving around in the world. For example, if I was invited to your event and I told you I was coming but didn't because I ended up sick, either/or thinking would have me say to you, "*I wanted to come to your party, but I was sick*" instead of saying "*I wanted to come to your party AND I was sick.*" See, both things are true. I wanted to come to the party AND I was sick. One does not disqualify the other.

The laws of attraction and contagion plus 'AND movements' provide the foundation for bringing our spiritual selves into the classroom. Spirituality is defined as "our most authentic relationships to self, others, the universe, and the transcendent" (Jones, 2005, p. 1) that influences and impacts how we interact with the world around us. Spirituality is often equated with religion and morality, which causes heated debates inside and outside learning environments. For most of us, we work for and with institutions that keep spirituality outside learning spaces. Again, this is because spirituality is seen as synonymous with religion and in this country, we supposedly have separation of Church and State. Spirituality is not religion and is not governed by any religious dogma. Spirituality is about our inner selves, the sacredness we all have inside of us. Spirituality is our consciousness, our sense of self and the way we receive and react to outside stimuli. Spirituality is our innate way of knowing that takes into consideration our intuition, gut feelings, sacredness, connectedness to others and the world, and the mysterious; those things we cannot easily define or explain. Religion is exclusive where spirituality is inclusive because we ALL have a spiritual self, and that self is connected to everything and everyone around us. We are not excluded from the earth. We are a part of it. So, for simplicity, I will define spirituality *as our innate way of knowing and that knowing predates all religion*. Certain religions may embrace innate ways of knowing but for most dominant religions that knowing comes from a higher power. Hopefully this helps you to see that spirituality is not religion. Remember those 'AND movements'. You can be spiritual AND religious, but they are not synonymous.

Spirituality is the foundation of our whole being. According to bell hooks (2001), "spiritual life is first and foremost about commitment to a way of thinking and behaving that honors principles of inner-being and interconnectedness" (p. 77). We know that when one area of our lives (our mental health for example) is 'ill' it affects other areas of our being as well, like our physical selves. In educational and learning settings, spirituality refers to "no more—and no less—than a deep connection between student, teacher and subject—a connection so honest, vital, and vibrant that it cannot help but be intensely relevant" (Jones, 2005, p. 1). This deep connection is carried out into the 'real world' wherever the students go and whoever they interact with. Spirituality has a rippling effect that once ignited, continues to make lasting connections. There's that law of contagion again. Robert Nash (2002) writes in *Spirituality, Ethics, Religion, and Teaching: A*

Professor's Journey, that "religion is the institution; spirituality is the personal. Religion is what we do with others; spirituality is what we do within ourselves" (p. 166). Spirituality is the force that creates meaning in our lives; that helps us determine what matters most to us and orientates us into the world around us. Once we recognize our spirituality, we can empathize. Spirituality is what allows us to really see each other, to find commonalities, to feel that interconnectedness. It is the ability to learn with our eyes and hearts fully open. Empathy allows us to ask, *"what is my experience, what are the connections between myself and others, and are those connections being honored?"* Spirituality "has to do with what values we hold dear, our sense of who we are and where we come from, our beliefs about why we are here, the meaning and purpose in our life and work, and our sense of connectedness to each other and the world around us" (Astin, 2004, p. 34). Spirituality considers the whole person. If we are not fully self-aware of who we are and what matters to us, we will not be able to understand others and effectively resolve conflict. Spirituality informs our other ways of innate knowing such as intuition, inspiration, and creation. There is an important mantra I live by which is *as above, so below* which means what affects our outer selves also affects our inner selves. Or in a broader sense, what affects the individual affects the collective.

For real transformative learning to take place, we must show up as our whole selves. Academia has perfected the art of dissecting folx and leaving only what it constitutes as acceptable ways of teaching and learning. Academia likes to compartmentalize. Transformative teaching is a spiritual act. By learning something new, we are literally creating something from nothing. If we teach and learn as whole beings with our spirituality intact, it means that our innate ways of knowing inform and support new information and concepts. We learn from a place that accepts what we already know and values that knowledge. This circles back to the idea that we are all experts of our own lived experiences. That innate knowing is that expertise and teaching with empathy not only recognizes its value but encourages its incorporation into the learning process. One misconception about incorporating spirituality into learning environments is that "any way of knowing that requires subjective involvement between the knower and the known is regarded as primitive, unreliable, and even dangerous" (Palmer, 2003, p.52). Spiritual knowledge, according to Melanie Goodchild (2020), is the "most denigrated knowledge in western traditions. Spiritual knowledge is somehow inferior and yet that is the most profound and important type of knowledge [for our ceremonies]". Teaching with our whole selves, with our spirituality front and center, is a more authentic and empathic way to connect and build connections with our students. We need to move past our fear of spirituality and break down the barriers that prevent us from making real connections. Inside academia, we place a lot of emphasis and power into the scientific method (and for good reason) so much so that if we want to explore other types of relationships to scholarship, expertise, and knowledge, it risks our very reputations. Reputation is what matters to the academic institution NOT the impact teaching has on learners, especially not the inner world of learners. As Robin Wall Kimmerer (2013) writes in *Braiding Sweetgrass: Indigenous Wisdom, Scientific Knowledge, and the Teachings of Plants*, "they've [scientists] been so conditioned to be skeptical of even the hardest of hard data that bending their minds toward theories that are verified with the expected graphs or equations is tough. Couple that with the unblinking assumption that science has cornered the market on truth and there's not much room for discussion" (p. 160).

What if we taught from a place that recognizes classrooms and sites of learning as sacred spaces? What if inside these sacred spaces we taught holistically and empathetically? What if we were comfortable being vulnerable in front of our students? *Sacred* is another word that becomes synonymous with religion. Spaces can be sacred and secular just as spaces can be sacred and religious. Sacred is simply something that is worthy of awe, and respect. Sacredness is not solely reserved for higher powers. Objects, places, and even texts can be considered sacred. Mass consensus does not dictate sacredness. Everyday folx can have places within their own communities and backyards that are sacred to them. Sacred can be extremely personal and individualized. Most folx have something sacred inside their homes whether they define it specifically as sacred. Folx may have altars or shrines set up in their homes to honor loved ones by displaying photographs, flowers, trinkets, and other personal items. The sacredness of these altars allows them to feel close to those who have passed on. All of us crave and seek out the sacred. The difference is what we define as sacred and how we incorporate it into our lives. Deep and critical learning is a sacred act worthy of awe and respect. Therefore, the classroom (or whatever learning is happening) is sacred. According to Steven Glazer (1999) sacredness as it relates to learning, is "rooting education in the practices of openness, attentiveness to experience, and sensitivity to the world" (p. 11-12).

Spirituality and spiritual knowledge are innate ways of knowing and shouldn't be put aside during our teaching. Some folx might see this as an invitation to recruit or proselytize but what I'm actually advocating is teaching with the whole self—for showing up authentically as the spiritual beings we all are. There is real momentum behind this idea of incorporating other forms of knowledge into research and learning. The DataCenter provides excellent frameworks for making space for spiritual and experiential learning which seeks to move past our rigid notion of what defines knowledge and expertise. Our current learning system relies heavily on mainstream and institutional knowledge which is information created by research professionals mostly outside of the communities they conduct research on/for. These information systems are what most of us are familiar with, scholarly articles, magazines, newspapers, cable network news and local news channels. Of course, mainstream and institutional knowledge is not without bias as it is built upon the same systemic oppression that our entire country was founded on. One does not have to look long to see that most of the scholarship produced in this country is by white males. Our organization systems, algorithms that make search engines like Google run, the publishing platform and peer review processes are all gatekeepers that let in the status quo and shut out marginalized voices. If mainstream and institutional knowledge only include certain folx then marginalized communities are not getting their stories, experiences, or knowledge shared with wider audiences. The ways of knowing that fall outside the accepted definitions of scholarship and expertise will never reach the same publishing platforms. Our white, westernized, colonizer definitions of scholarship and expertise are extremely biased, racist, and oppressive. White folx do not hold more expertise than non-white folx (although we push this false narrative), which is why we need to make space for other ways of knowing inside learning spaces. We need to validate and facilitate other ways of sharing information and knowledge. We need to redefine what scholarship is and what an expert looks like.

Cultural and spiritual knowledge as well as experiential knowledge are valid forms of knowing. If we implement a framework that considers all three of these ways of knowing, we create inclusive learning spaces. If we see each of these categories as equally important and legitimate, we not only lead with empathy but create exciting opportunities for scholarship and research. Imagine what students could learn if we broadened the definition of knowledge. Imagine if we allowed students the space to ask spiritual questions that attempted to answer what is meaning, what is identity, what is responsibility? When these questions are ignored and silenced, they create disease (illness) inside the body. A severance is created between our physical selves and our innate spirituality which in turn creates a barrier between us and those around us. In education, we place too much emphasis on grades, memorization, credits earned, and busy work. This hyperfocus allows zero time for students to do the inner work. Spirituality is that inner work that can "raise consciousness, stimulate awareness, foster creativity and imagination, connect us to grander issues of purpose and meaning and facilitate connection with that which animates us" (Tolliver cited in (Jones, 2005, p. 6). The spiritual work that involves the development of "affective skills such as empathy, cooperation, leadership, interpersonal understanding, and self-understanding" (Astin, 2004, p. 36) are not part of our pedagogical repertoire. When we take a more holistic approach to teaching and learning, we recognize and appreciate that to be human is to not only to think but to feel.

Cultural, spiritual, and experiential knowledge are just as important as mainstream and institutional knowledge. When I teach, I enter into an agreement with students that recognizes:

- **That proximity to power** is established by whomever is positioned at the front of the room.
- **That expertise is for everyone,** and we are all experts at something.
- **That you go with you** and that your biases, experiences, and emotions come with you into the classroom.
- **That innate creativity** we are all born with plays a critical role in our learning.

Healing

Spirituality is what heals. Healing "is an attempt to put broken pieces back together and dissolve layers of debris that block us from operating at our highest selves" (Karnatz, 2022, p. 20). Healing cannot happen if we are not equipped to reflect on the larger questions of life. Melanie Goodchild (personal communication, September 29, 2020) states, "healing work must be part of system change work and love." A cursory look into our education systems shows us how diseased our institutions truly are. Increasingly, education is transactional and operated with a business mindset. Higher education is bloated with upper administration hard pressed to justify their six-figure salaries while students are pushed along through programs to increase funding, enrollment numbers, rankings, and whatever else the institution finds valuable. Education in general is fixated on test scores, rankings, and popularity polls and not on the inner lives of students, faculty, and the community-at-large. This creates disease, a rot from the inside out that makes true and meaningful learning almost impossible to justify without a higher price tag. I hear all the time how students lack critical thinking skills, and it is no wonder. How can we ask them to critically think and evaluate the outside world if they have not had the opportunity to look inward? From the moment students step into kindergarten, the spiritual aspects of their being are weeded out. We make sure of it with standardized testing and the loss of art and music programs. A liberal arts education is facing extinction.

Mass media and the Alt-Right like to equate a liberal arts education with socialism, communism, and anarchy instead of seeing its true value. It is in liberal arts where students have the best chance of exploring and (re)discovering their inner self, their spirituality, and the sacredness that builds empathy and provides a connection to others. It's within liberal arts where creativity, intuition, and play are fostered and encouraged. It's where healing begins and disease is managed. When unnecessary barriers prevent students from taking liberal arts classes, we divorce them from their true, innate selves and force them to fragment and separate from their spiritual selves. When we put all our money and energies into programs that churn out the most workers for capitalism, we do not graduate well-rounded, spiritual, curious, and self-aware folx but automatons who have learned over time to bury their true selves and embrace the status quo. We have caused our students to dissociate, and our educational system is to blame.

I completely understand the financial barriers to a liberal arts education. Most students do not have the financial luxury to dabble in different disciplines. Many students enroll in community colleges and trade schools to fast-track a career so they can better their lives. But dabbling is where students will uncover what they are truly passionate about. Most students will never take an art course or a creative writing class and so they will live their lives thinking they either hate art and/or suck at writing creatively. They never had the opportunity to be proven wrong and this is one of the reasons why we all feel so disconnected from ourselves and each other. I cannot stress this enough, creativity heals. Creativity is essential for deep learning. We need to find ways to bring this healing work into the classroom in whatever way we can. If the institutions we sell our souls to won't provide the space and financial means for our students to graduate as holistic people, then we must do what we can one instruction session at a time. We owe it to our students to show them that spirituality, creativity and learning can coexist, and that existence is crucial to their wellbeing.

Embracing our spirituality alone won't heal what is ill. Educational reform is necessary from elementary school all the way to doctoral programs. Spirituality, sacredness in teaching and learning, and empathy can start the healing process if we are willing to put ourselves out there and take a risk. And it is a risk. For some of us, a significant risk. I am currently in a tenure track position and must prove my worth every year to keep my job. Taking too big of risks jeopardizes my chances of staying employed but if I don't take chances with the way I teach and interact with students, I risk losing myself. I recognize that I come from a place of privilege to even say that losing myself would have a greater impact than losing my employment because I can always find another job. I'm not advocating for folx to go out and blow up their professional lives, but I am suggesting starting tiny fires where we can. Everything starts out on the micro level so any kind of change made will eventually ripple out into the macro. Healing must start with us, with our spiritual selves. We cannot connect fully and authentically with others without using our innate knowledge. We won't ever be able to solve all the big institutional issues in this country like systemic oppression, police brutality, the killing of the planet, and mass shootings if we don't stop and embrace our spiritual selves. But embracing is not enough. ACTION must follow. How will we take what we have learned and move it outward? How will we be agents of change in the classroom? How can those of us who have privilege, especially white privilege, use it to call out and call in?

The one place that can answer some of these questions is our educational system. We can provide the spaces for healing to happen right inside the classroom. Small shifts can be just as important as the seismic ones. What matters is that the shifts come from a place of empathy and authenticity and room is made for students to investigate their inner lives and apply that knowledge inside the classroom. "We have so much more to give from a more holistic place when we prioritize self-awareness and self-development" (Karnatz, 2022, p. 22). It's time to bring back the whole self and move away from transactional learning. What we need is an educational system that embraces spirituality, creativity, and experiential knowledge. When we teach and learn this way, we heal not just ourselves but the system we find ourselves imprisoned in. "Putting focus on healing yourself is deeply value to the community" (Karnatz, 2022, p. 22). We won't be able to do this work alone. It's time to sit down and really think about strategic partnerships, those folx and departments that can move the work we want to do forward. We must find our people. They are out there. Our people show up in all areas of our lives. When we start viewing ourselves as whole spiritual beings and not fragmented pieces, we see our people more clearly. They might not be in our department or even at our institution. We need to build bridges. We need to go out into the community to share our ideas and listen to others. We need to take turns lifting each other up so that everyone can see beyond the ivory tower.

Water Activities

Teaching and Learning Empathy Statement (for correspondence)

One of the best ways to practice empathy is putting it front and center on our syllabus and/or course documents, and email signatures. The syllabus is an accountability piece between us and our students. This is THE place to show empathy and demonstrate how the class will support each other as whole beings. This is one I created and currently use:

> I recognize that while teaching and learning is important, it must take a backseat to our own lives which include those whom we care about and for. Your identities and how they intersect are impacted by the immediate environment and our current political landscape. Show up authentically when, how and where you can. No one is penalized for what they can give. My role is to assist in the building of a class community that honors our experiences, thoughts, feelings, and expertise. Yes, you have expertise.
>
> I recognize that folx celebrate various holidays and events in a myriad of ways and I respect each and every person's journey. If you find yourself preparing for a holiday and/or event

that falls during one of the weeks you are in this course, don't feel obligated to show up and do the work. There is always the following week or whenever life lets you circle back to it. Our journey around this rock is amazing and important. I see that and I see you.

With that said, I will challenge you in this course and you are accountable for the work assigned but it must never come at the expense of your health (spiritual, emotional, physical, and mental). Pushing ourselves past exhaustion serves no one except the wheels of capitalism and we will not feed this machine any more than absolutely necessary in this class.

Lastly, I recognize that I might slip up, forget something, or be late in presenting materials or grades to ya'll. I absolutely promise to show up authentically and own my mistakes and missteps.

These are my pledges to you.

Teaching holistically means allowing students the opportunity to step out momentarily if they need to achieve balance. It means moving forward despite the fear of being taken advantage of. We can't penalize the majority over a few students because nothing is gained by the students who are apt to take advantage. There is, however, tremendous gain for the students who need an empathy statement. I know there were students in my previous classes who took advantage of my kindness, and this has never stopped me from being empathetic and giving everyone the benefit of the doubt. I want to model the kind of behavior I wish educators had embodied when I was a student. I can only imagine how much more balanced I would have been if past educators had seen and treated me as a whole person and not just a body occupying a seat in the room.

I invite you to adopt an empathy statement into your work. We all benefit from these statements and commitments to one another. This worker bee is tired. I'm tired of knowing that if I died tomorrow, my institution would replace me within a few months' time. I'm not naïve. I know capitalism doesn't care about me and yet I still show up as my whole self, including the me that is burnt out. I need to know that my well-being matters to my colleagues because I spend most of my life with them at work. Until something changes (like the destruction of capitalism), my wellbeing is linked to my work environment. It's not that I love capitalism but rather I love my career so for me to shine and take up space, I need to take care of myself so I can do the work I am called to do.

Another way to use empathy accountability statements is in our email signatures. We don't need to write a vignette, but a few sentences about self-care and work balance gives folx the option to ignore our email until they have the bandwidth to engage. These statements are a gentle reminder to prioritize the limited time and energy we have. It gives folx agency to say 'no, this can wait' without creating superficial 'do or die' states of being. Here is my email signature adapted from a few I've seen circulating:

> Please know that I honor and respect personal boundaries around time, self-care, caregiving, and time off. If you receive an email from me during a time where you are engaged in any of the above, please protect your time and wait to respond until you are working. Always try to prioritize joy over email when you can. You matter. Always.

I also have one on my personal email that serves as a mindfulness activity.

> There is so much love and loss in the world and I would like to take a few breaths to acknowledge all the folx who, for known and unknown reasons, succumbed to suicide. May their painful absence in our lives be a powerful presence for change.

These signatures are a simple way to show empathy. Any time we can gently push back against capitalism and its incessant need for us to be engaged 24/7 is a good thing. When we interact with others from a place of understanding, we shift proximities to power and lay groundwork for building a more balanced and equitable way to exist and be in service with each other. Try adding a little message to your email signatures. I guarantee someone will receive your message and internalize those much-needed sentences. Even small moments of peace and reprieve are beautiful.

Accountability and Learning Agreements

No one likes busywork. I admit that throughout my graduate program I routinely skipped required readings. Like many students in university,

I was attending graduate school full-time while working a full-time job and a part-time job to make ends meet. I did not have time to read all the things and I had even less time to spend doing mindless work with little to no pay-off. I've sat through many classes (in-person and online) where there is a huge disconnect between the course objectives and assignments. Honestly, research papers are not always the best way to gauge a student's understanding of course materials. Research papers have value, but I wrote too many during my academic career that did not have any lasting impact on my life. I would be hard pressed to tell you what more than 98% of them were about. Research papers are easy to assign yet they are not the most engaging to write (or read). Educators everywhere are burnt out. With increased workloads and student-to-teacher ratios with declining salaries and professional development opportunities, there is little to no time to critically evaluate and redesign our courses. Throw in standards, frameworks, and standardized testing and you have even less of a chance of throwing out research papers and miscellaneous busywork. Believe me, I get it, but something must change, and soon, if we want students to really engage in the learning process and take those transferable skills with them out into the world.

We need to understand why students disengage and help them become accountable for their part in the learning agreement. When we enter the classroom, we create an unspoken learning agreement. We agree to share knowledge and skills with the students and the students agree to pay attention (as best they can), synthesize and apply the new information and/or skills with what they already know. We all agree to ask questions and answer whichever ones we can with as much honesty and knowledge as we possess. The problem lies oftentimes in the material and presentation of that material. If given the chance, the average person will do the bare minimum to get by so when we engage in a learning agreement with students, they need to know what the added value is and how this will impact their current situation. So often when librarians are asked to speak to students about the research process, there is no specific piece of research assigned yet. This disconnect makes it hard for students to see the value in learning research skills, and so many students will falsely believe that they suck at research because of it.

How do we meet the expectations of faculty while also building a connection with the students so that they find relevance and value in the material we are presenting? What if we are called into the classroom where there is no assignment yet, or worse, there is no research component at all? The key is linking the material to something community-specific while highlighting the specific database/journal/whatever the faculty needs us to go over. Personally, I care less about the specific resource, as they come and go, and more about the actual skills and techniques of research. Let's be real here. Students lose access to subscription databases the moment they graduate. Many students will go into fields where these databases are cost prohibitive. So yeah, it is helpful to know how to search CINAHL but at the end of the day, I want students to know how to search. Anywhere. Therefore, I focus my energy on HOW to find scholarly content and evaluate it because most students are going to use Google (Scholar). We all know it. In fact, even after I show them subscription databases that their professor wants them to use, most students will go back to searching Google almost immediately, even during the instruction session itself. Why? Because we are creatures of habit and like to use materials and tools that we are comfortable with. Most students are happy with the results they obtain from Google (Scholar) even if they don't understand page ranking or sponsored content.

Instead of devoting most of the time to how to research a particular resource, I talk about the how: the strategies, tricks, and techniques that are applicable to what they are searching. The skills are the same and to me, this is the learning opportunity and the real takeaway. How we can hold students accountable to our learning agreements is by discussing the places they already search and talking about the ins and outs of those resources. Remember the research conversation I talked about in Chapter 3? Pair this with community-specific hands-on activities and students will be more apt to pay attention because they can see how it directly relates to their own lives. Research is a conversation and it's also about building connections between things. To move beyond the learning agreement into the accountability piece, here are some hands-on learning activities to try:

- Have students read a quick article and then recite what they remember aloud to the class. This builds skills in getting to the heart of a resource, to determine the main points and synthesize information. What we remember is what resonates the most with us. Shaun McNiff (1998) in his book *Trust the Process: An Artist's Guide to Letting Go*, "drawing from memory helps the process of distillation because we do not retain everything. Forgetting plays an important role in extracting the marrow from the situation"(p. 108).

- Have students situate an assigned resource into an ongoing scholarly conversation. For instance, if the class is assigned to read a particular resource, have them search for background information on the author, when the resource was written (what was going on in the world during the time of publication), allusions, or common knowledge that the author assumes readers know. See if students can find a few reviews of the work to help put the text into context. This not only helps reinforce the importance of evaluation but also teaches them how to use databases to search for literature reviews and critiques. Most importantly, it illustrates just how important context is.

- Expanding on the previous activity, students can research the author(s) of the assigned text. One of the most difficult aspects of reading resources for research is knowing how to interact with the text. So often students don't see themselves in the work. They have no idea why the resource was written or what impact it had on the author or community-at-large. Having students research authors helps situate the text so that they can understand what an author was pushing back against, what point-of-view they had, why the author wrote the piece and who the author thought the audience of the work would be. It also shows who else cited the work and where that piece of research had the most impact. This kind of activity helps students really see that all research is an ongoing conversation and no matter where you enter it, evaluation and investigation of resources is important.

- Have students help design assignments and rubrics that allow for deeper connections with their research process. When students not only help design an assignment but the rubric which outlines how they will be evaluated, more ownership and pride is taken in the work they create. Working with the faculty member to experiment in this type of student engagement might be a challenge at first, but we might be surprised to see who is ready to do something different if we only ask.

Mindfulness Movement

Other ways we can help students overcome their anxiety about research is by adding a mindfulness activity, and/or creative time in class so that they get a chance to create movement. Movement is an excellent way to shift energy especially if students are feeling stuck.

I've given students 5–10-minute breaks in which they can walk around the classroom, stretch, or walk around the library. I've even instructed them to mindfully walk to the end of the floor by walking as slowly as possible so that they are aware of every step they take. I've given creative breaks where we set aside our research to color on coloring sheets I provided or doodle on blank sheets of paper. I've even had students sit in silence with their eyes closed just to recenter themselves. Music is another powerful tool to share with students. I've been in classrooms where professors will stop lecturing to play a song or piece of music to shift the energy in the classroom. Sometimes thinking outside the box and doing something unexpected is enough of a jolt to reawaken our senses.

The Work

Reflection Questions

- What fears and hesitations do you have with bringing spirituality into the classroom? How might you overcome those fears?
- How does the current educational system prevent you from authentically showing up in the classroom?
- What pieces of yourself do you have to leave outside academia in order to uphold the status quo?
- Who are your people? How can you build a bridge to them if one does not already exist?

Reflection Activities

- Create your own teaching and learning with an empathy statement and consider implementing it in one or all of the courses you teach.
- Create an empathy email signature. What do you want others to know, *really know*, when they receive an email from you?
- Create a mindfulness activity you could use in your instruction sessions if you see that students are drifting off or worse, nodding off.

Chapter 7

Fire
Creation, Transformation

Create as if your life depended on it.

I believe critical creativity is essential to deep learning. Critical creativity is students "using creative expression to demonstrate deeper thinking and the nuances of understanding content" (Burvall & Ryder, 2017, p. 8). When critical creativity is used to "make connections, transform knowledge, and articulate the reasons behind their creative choices, learning becomes more sticky, meaningful, and authentic" (Burvall & Ryder, 2017). Critical creativity is not art for art's sake but dedicated time and space to deconstruct and reconstruct ideas, information, knowledge, and resources. It's intentional play meant to spark new ideas through a creative lens. In a broader sense, critical creativity is "the need to explore how the mechanisms imposed by cultural hegemony and colonialism have affected the[it] four faces: the personal face, the historical face, the political face, and the sacred face" (Tisdell & Tolliver, 2003, p. 371) and that in reclaiming these four faces through art, music, and creative play, social transformations occur.

Critical creativity is a vital piece of scholarship and one that is often misused and misunderstood. Critical creativity is not an easy classroom filler. On the contrary, critical creativity uses both sides of the brain to make sense of the world around us. Before I go any further, I want to state that everyone is creative. Let me say it a little louder for the folx in the back, EVERYONE IS CREATIVE. Usually at a very young age we are made aware that our creative work is being judged. Some of us decided to walk away from creativity because we did not feel good enough. Some of us, whether we internalized that criticism or not, pushed onward and stayed on the creative course. So, I get the fear that rises in students when they hear critical creativity. I understand the urge to shut down when asked to be creative. Suddenly creativity is synonymous with talent. Sure, there are students who are talented at creating things, but talent is not a prerequisite for doing creative works because we can all create something significant if given the space and 'permission' to do so. None of us, including those we teach, will ever know what we are truly capable of creating until we give ourselves permission to do so. Throughout this chapter I hope to convince you to give yourself and your students that permission.

There is a common resistance to critical creativity and self-expression, and I have seen this play out in every single classroom where I have introduced creative elements into the learning process. We all fear judgment, especially around something we already falsely believe we are not good at. We fear that the finished product simply won't be 'good enough' before we even know what the end product can look like. We convinced ourselves we are not smart enough, talented enough, brave enough or whatever enough to do the thing that requires creativity. We are not 'creative in THAT way,' in whatever THAT way might be. We are quick to dismiss something outside our comfort circles. We fear that through critical creativity we might reveal too much about ourselves and that would require a level of vulnerability we are not willing to show. From young college students to senior citizens, this resistance is so deeply rooted that most students do not believe me when I say that by the time the creative thing is finished, they will have rediscovered their joy in making something. (For what it's worth, so far, I have not been wrong). Play is necessary. If we allow students to believe creativity is an unproductive waste of our time, we let capitalism win. Our students remain disembodied and disconnected from themselves and each other because they don't see value in their creative selves.

Let's circle back to the idea of talent. Society has a specific and extremely narrow definition of what a creative person looks like. This definition supports the dominant narrative we have talked about throughout this book. Even creative spaces have dominant narratives and systematic oppression. Society loves its labels and enjoys placing labels on all of us which situates us in one box or thing. Society does not like a crossover or the blending of things. Society loves itself a binary. Remember, binary thinking is one of the aspects of white supremacy and capitalism. We all have intersecting identities and are more than one thing at any given time. So, you can be a researcher and an artist. You can be a doctor and a creative writer. You can be a mechanic and a creative person. Part of critical creativity is smashing the binary that keeps us confined to one and only one thing at a time. Research is hard and fun. Learning is challenging and creative. In the Western world, we have separated creativity from other aspects of our lives. Instead, we put boundaries around our work that keep play out, but creativity belongs in all spaces. Creative ways of looking at the world allow us to embrace multiple truths and their intersections. When we place one truth above the others, we support dominant narratives and oppressive ways of making meaning. We shut the door on empathy. If we instead bring critical creativity into every space of learning, we will see true transformation happen as students remember and reacquaint themselves with the creative spirit that resides in all of them. Critical creativity happens by being creative. We must do the thing in order to do the thing. There is tremendous energy in stepping outside our comfort circles and we need to harness that energy for 'AND movements'.

Critical creativity and the research processes share a lot in common. Both have false starts, frustrations, feelings of being overwhelmed and anxious, and serendipitous discoveries, breakthroughs, and failures. The process of creativity and information seeking are fluid, relational, and organic. Both processes are building blocks where one thing emerges from another. Everything is in partnership with each other if we allow it. One of the most powerful aspects of bringing in critical creativity is the ability for students to "understand complex concepts through the remixing of ideas and information" (Burvall & Ryder, 2017, p. 16) through an element of play. Simply put, critical creativity is not always about creating something new, but rather taking information and remixing it in a different way so that a more critical and comprehensive level of understanding can be achieved. Say we have a toaster that we are curious about, so we take it apart and see what we find. Through our research we add new pieces to the toaster to make it something better, accessible, and/or exciting. We can talk about our learning process because we have in-depth knowledge and understanding of what the toaster was and what it is now. We have a connection, a story, a narrative around the dismantling and reconstruction of the toaster. Because we have a personal connection to our toaster, we can talk about how we feel regarding our discoveries and creation. This is what critical creativity looks like. There are ways to bring critical creativity into the classroom that do not require great lengths of time or actually dismantling a toaster.

Each of the activities I mention in this chapter takes time and practice and so flexibility is important. This is not to discourage you from taking on critical creativity but to reiterate that creativity is not less rigorous or scholarly than other types of activities. Critical creativity is fun and challenging, meaningful and transformative. I have seen many professors attempt to implement critical creativity activities to fill up class time or move away from research papers without any solid relationship between research and the creative project. Critical creativity is rooted in the remixing and reimagining of ideas and concepts. It will not work without intention. When thinking about incorporating critical creativity into the spaces you occupy, you should be intentional. Art for art's sake is beautiful and has its place but it is not critical creativity. One practical way to implement critical creativity into instruction is through mini-assignments or mini-activities. These are low stakes that do not take up a lot of class time and involve less overall commitment. Remember the occupation drawings that literally illustrate unconscious bias? This is a perfect example of a quick way to implement critical creativity into any classroom. These activities are what I call 'veiled learning' where folx assume we are doing a fun, random activity without being consciously aware they are learning something. So many of the critical creativity activities I outline in this chapter fall under veiled learning. I've done them enough times know that not only do they work but they are immensely enjoyable. So enjoyable in fact, that some students will continue doing the thing well after the class is over.

Before I get into the details of critical creativity activities, I want to tell you about the class that started it all. In 2017 I taught a learning community course for sophomores at Simmons University. I developed my course around the ideas of information spectrums, personal narrative writing and zines. As a research and instruction librarian, I know what a hard sell research is. In my experience, students are always kind and appreciative when I come into their classrooms to talk about research techniques, but I know it isn't the most exciting thing to learn about. So much of what I teach in one-shot instruction sessions is situated around a specific database or resource, usually at the professor's request. At the time it didn't leave a whole lot of room for me to get creative. I have since moved past this barrier. So, when I was presented with the opportunity to teach the learning community course, I knew how I wanted to teach the research process. The veiled learning of this course was the information spectrums component. Through this lens, we explored the importance of personal narrative writing, storytelling, knowledge systems, meaning making, what makes an expert, and zines as scholarship. This course changed my career and teaching trajectory forever.

Class sessions were structured around student-centered learning as well as critical creativity activities, assigned zines and scholarly articles. Early on the students were asked to identify a community they belonged to that is often surrounded by misconceptions and stereotypes. The assignments, in-class activities and discussion questions were scaffolded to prepare them for researching their communities. I anticipated that their communities would be hard to research based on semantics and validity in the eyes of Western society. For a few students this was eye-opening and led to justified anger towards classification systems and scholarship in general. For others it validated what they already suspected. Overall, everyone walked away empathetic to each other's community and the role they played inside of it. The course allowed opportunities for the students to see and hear one another.

All the assignments and activities informed their final project, which was a zine. We co-created the project guidelines and rubric for grading. Their finished zines were incredible. On the last day of class, everyone, including me, presented their zine. We sat in a circle (which we did in every class meeting) and talked. We discussed what we struggled with, why we made the artistic decisions we made (font, color schemes, images selected, etc.), what lit us up during the process and where we saw our zine fitting into scholarly conversations around our communities. Representation matters and for several students this was the very first time they were truthfully represented in something published. That is powerful. I realized early in the semester that more time was needed to work on our zine in class. We all struggled finding time to be creative and write. Even when we found time, we felt guilty, feeling like we should be spending our time on more 'academic' work. All this information allowed me to pivot and restructure the course a few weeks in so that we had time at the end of each class to work on our zines. Students could work on the writing pieces, the research, or the actual cut-and-paste. It was entirely up to them. Each student took turns selecting the music we would listen to while we worked. Adding the musical component was another way to build community and learn more about each other as we shared creative space.

Each class session followed a similar structure. We began with a two-minute portrait drawing. I adapted this from Linda Barry's(2014) *Syllabus*. These portraits served many purposes. On a logistical level it was how I took attendance. After students created their portraits, I collected them and did not return them until the last day of class. This two-minute activity put us all in the creative mindset. I did the portraits along with them as well as any guests that attended the class. There were all kinds of feelings at first about the portraits. Some students were convinced they could not draw, and others had no idea what they really looked like. This last concern sounds absurd but when you really sit and think about the structure and lines of your face, you might realize you haven't really paid much attention. Throughout the semester students found their groove and their own unique style of drawing themselves. Eventually I learned their artistic style so well that I knew who the portrait was of before I even read the name on the back. A beautiful thing happened over the course of the semester. A freedom of expression took hold that was evident in their portraits. What started out controlled and mechanical ended up being playful and full of whimsy. On the last day of class I returned to each student their stack of portraits so they could see the progress they made in building their creative confidence. The 'I'm not creative' mindset that took hold at the beginning of our time together had all but faded. The portraits allowed us to slow down and practice mindfulness. Doing portrait drawings at the start of class allowed for more creative play and curiosity during the class session. We learned that if we could be mindful for two minutes, perhaps we could practice mindfulness a bit longer somewhere else in our day.

After portraits, we moved into group-led discussions. On the first day of class students got into groups and chose which weeks they wanted to lead. Each group discussion had to critique the week's readings, which always included a scholarly article or two and a zine. They had to discuss why these resources were paired with each other, what themes they discovered as well as questions that surfaced. These questions were then presented to the class for open discussion. Watching each group teach to and learn from their peers was exciting and inspiring. I learned so much from them just in how they interpreted the texts and applied what they learned to real life examples. I only interjected in these discussions if things were stalled or if questions seemed too lofty to answer. Group-led discussions were the perfect segue into my presentation, which always involved information spectrum concepts. Whether it was dominant narratives, semantics and controlled vocabulary, algorithmic biases or definitions of expertise, it all came back to how there are many ways of knowing and that scholarship takes many forms and they, the students, are scholars and experts in their own right.

Next came our critical creativity activity. I spent a great deal of time creating these activities and pairing them with specific lessons. If they could dissect complex ideas and theories, move the pieces around and reassemble them into something new, then it was physical proof that they understood the lesson. The activities modeled the learning process: being flexible, seeing things from different perspectives, cultivating empathy and/or focusing on 'AND movements'. I took inspiration from everything and kept a notebook of ideas to implement. Some of them were successes and others kind of flopped, but my goal was to keep moving and learning.

I no longer teach this course AND I still incorporate a lot of these critical creativity activities into my one-shot instructions. Things like two-minute portrait drawings, student-led discussions, and non-dominant handwriting (I'll get to that in a moment) can be applied in these sessions. While they might seem to have nothing to do with information literacy or what you are called into the classroom to teach, I assure you that students will not only appreciate doing something unexpected but will learn to see information differently. This opens the possibility for a creative and curious mind. I am sharing with you the activities that worked. I recognize that each community and institution is different as well as the students we teach. Feel free to adapt and change these activities to fit your own needs. Add to them, remix them. I've tried to list these activities by how much time and resources are needed to do them properly. However, anything and everything can be modified to meet your and your students' unique needs.

Fire Activities

Pillars of Support

This activity allows students to visually see what holds them up. I start by showing images of the temples for Athena and Nefertiti and the Malta Megalith. What I want students to see is that despite most of the temple being in ruins, the pillars still stand. These pillars provided support for the entire structure and have stood the test of time. I pair these images with a quote from the zine *Small Magic* by Hannah (2005) that states, "to fight for my creativity, my right to write, for my voice, and my courage to defend the vulnerable flickering flame in me, that little burning desire to create" (p. 2) is to protect your power. I ask students to imagine their body as a temple that guards their inner light and to ask themselves, "what strengths support and protect my inner light from outside forces that want to extinguish my power?" The students then draw their pillars of strength. Some students draw actual temples and label each pillar while others draw circles that contain their strengths, displaying an aerial view. There is no right or wrong way to conceptualize this. The goal is to not only show how strong each of the students are but to remind them that when their light begins to flicker, they can call upon their pillars to hold them up. The pillars are a reminder that the courage to tell their stories, to be present as their authentic selves, and to honor themselves already resides inside them.

I've taught variations of this activity including having students list things (people, places, objects, etc.) that support them and the work they do. The possibilities are endless, and the point of the activity always remains the same. We are not alone. Another beautiful thing about this activity is visually seeing how their pillars change over time. What holds them up today might not next year and that's okay. It's one way to visually see growth and transformation through their experiences and struggles.

Non-dominant Hand

We live in a society that rushes us with a scarcity mindset that convinces us we are on a tight deadline and must do all the things yesterday. Be productive! Don't rest! You can sleep when you are dead! When we operate in a scarcity mindset, we never get the chance to deeply think about the work we are doing and the perspectives we hold about that work. One activity I have done with students is asking them to write about their research proposal with their non-dominant hand. By using our non-dominant hand, we are forced to slow down and really pay attention to our writing. In fact, we are forced to pay attention to each individual letter in a way that we haven't since we first learned to write. We take writing for granted. Our brains are working at lightning speed and our hands are writing or typing as fast as they can to keep up. Most of us never think about it. It's a mindless activity. Writing with our non-dominant shifts our perspectives as we become more mindful of our thought and writing processes. The students literally have to think about every single letter in every single word they commit to paper and in response they weed out unnecessary words. This weeding is an excellent way to practice writing that is specific and concise in getting their main points across. There's that veiled learning again.

This activity can be used in brainstorming sessions, explaining a topic or resource, introducing an idea or concept, or something as low key as writing the origins of their names. Using their non-dominant hand, students slow down and become mindful of writing and listening to their inner voice. Almost every time I have used this activity, the students loved it. Not only was it fun, but they appreciated the unexpected gift of specificity in writing.

Personally, I use the nondominant hand activity whenever I am stuck creatively. It helps sort out my thoughts and feelings by providing me with the opportunity to slow down. I keep a smashbook (more on this later) where what looks like scribbles are actually my nondominant handwriting through a creative block.

Memes

Memes are an entertaining way to summarize ideas, feelings, and learning objectives. I mean, who doesn't love a good meme! There are numerous websites that students can use to create memes although my personal favorite is https://imgflip.com/memegenerator. It's fun and super easy. Memes are a great way to personalize information, so it makes perfect sense to bring this activity into the classroom. Here are a few examples of how I use memes in my instruction sessions:

- Have students create a meme summarizing their research topic.
- Have students create a meme summarizing what they learned in the instruction session.
- Have students create a meme summarizing how their research is going.
- Have students create a meme summarizing how they are feeling right now.

I cannot tell you how many amazing memes have been created during this activity! Most students are excited to try their hand at creating a meme. Again, who doesn't love a good meme! The memes can be shared with the class, posted on the course page (inside Moodle, Canvas, Blackboard) and even incorporated into the students' actual research project. I've worked with professors who encouraged their students to incorporate their memes in their research paper, which makes the incentive to create an impactful meme even more important. With meme creation, students learn how to share information that is relatable to a general audience. It provides opportunities for students to practice summarizing main points, connecting with their audience, and sharing sometimes heavy-handed jargon and research data. A good meme can be an ice breaker, a talking point, and a way to create empathy and understanding with their audience. It's about finding what resonates and using that to convey complex thoughts and ideas in a way that is easily digestible.

Mantra Cards

One of my favorite critical creativity activities is creating mantra cards. Mantra cards are a method of self-reflection and consist of an image or images and text. There are numerous ways to approach mantra card making so it is an activity that most everyone can learn and do. I create them by hand using actual playing cards, but students can use digital resources if they are more comfortable doing so. To create mantra cards in an instruction setting you will need to provide pre-cut pieces of paper or a standard deck of cards. You can purchase decks of cards at yard sales and flea markets. It doesn't matter what the face of the cards look like as they will be covered up with original art. If students are creating cards by hand, you will need to bring some art supplies like colored pencils, markers, or gel pens.

The purpose of mantra cards is to provide a pathway for positive self-talk (intrapersonal rhetoric) and self-reflection. It's a deliberate interruption to the mindless negative thought patterns that occupy a lot of our students' minds. You can think of mantra cards as notes of encouragement or words of wisdom from students to themselves. How the student creates their card is entirely up to them. I've seen students create beautiful cards that were deeply personal. Some are witty while others are heartfelt and compassionate. There is no right or wrong way to create a mantra card, so the stakes are low. Before students create their card, I explain that the intention is to create a mantra, a reminder, so that when they are overwhelmed and/or feel like giving up, they see and hear their inner voice, which knows that they belong and that they matter. Mantra cards are a way students can show up for themselves when they need it most. Once the cards are created, students walk out of the classroom with a personal mantra they can use over and over again.

Here are two mantra cards that I have made over the last four years.

Fire

Figure 2   Images created by Dawn Rogers Stahura

Infographic Annabibs

I love annotated bibliographies as they are rigorous without the actual writing of a research paper. I see the value in writing research papers, but I think that they are assigned way too often. I've spoken with faculty who admit that they assign research papers because they don't know what else to have students do and lack the time to properly re-evaluate and restructure their courses. They want to do something different, but they are operating within that scarcity mindset. Because I don't give up easily, I've convinced several faculty over the years to abandon the research paper and assign instead critical annotated bibliographies instead. Students still do the research and use proper citation, but what makes annotated bibliographies *critical* is evaluating privilege through the ACT UP method. I wondered, though, if there was a way to combine critical creativity with the annotated bibliography. It was then that I came up with infographic annotated bibliographies or *infographic annabibs*, for short.

My working definition of *infographic annabibs* is the blending of the evaluation process and annotations with the creative design of info-graphics. The infographic is how the evaluation will be constructed and presented. To my knowledge *infographic annabibs* did not exist anywhere outside my own mind, and I was excited to implement it. My co-instructor, Dez Alaniz, and I assigned *infographic annabibs* to a course we were teaching, and the results amazed us! Our students (who were librarians) loved the assignment so much that several of them implemented *infographic annabibs* into their instruction sessions at their respective institutions. Since that time Dez and I have assigned *infographic annabibs* to all the courses we teach together. One frequent comment about the activity is how challenging it is. Oftentimes folx assume that critical creativity assignments are soft, easy learning when in fact, incorporating critical creativity is daunting because it asks students to use an entirely different skill set to approach their research. There is nothing easy about critical creativity. Fun, yes! Easy, no. I was thrilled to know that the assignment was challenging because it meant my faculty would have an easier time seeing *infographic annabibs* as legitimate assignments. Having this feedback from fellow librarians provided me with anecdotal evidence that I could take to faculty proving that the assignment was rigorous. So far this semester, one professor has assigned *infographic anabibs* in which students are required to annotate a resource from the required reading list. It's a way for students to do a deep dive into a resource of their choice while also being creative. I would love to see *infographic annabibs* implemented in a science course where critical creativity is often missing. Usually in the hard sciences, critical creativity is a hard sell as faculty simply don't see how it fits and what value it brings to the classroom. With *infographic annabibs*, it is a chance to blend visual elements with text to critically analyze and annotate a scholarly article. The applications of this activity seem endless. I can imagine students creating *infographic annabibs* and presenting them in a poster session type environment or passing them out as a mini literature review on important topics like climate change, police brutality, or health care disparities. Accessibility, in terms of language and layout, of *infographic annabibs* would broaden the potential audience of readers and provide an engaging entryway into student research.

Zines

I've been creating zines since the 1990s. As a young person growing up in the middle of nowhere Indiana, I didn't feel part of a community. I felt isolated, weird, and eccentric. I had a hard time making and keeping friends who really saw me and valued me for who I was. I attribute my successful transition from adolescence into young adulthood to my best friend, Barbie, and zines. Zines saved my life as they gave me a chance to read about other folx's issues and experiences that mirrored my own: folx who lived in different parts of the world and also felt isolated, weird, and eccentric. Young folx who were writing about their feelings and sharing them with strangers. It was brave and badass. My early zines were perzines (personal zines) that documented my experiences and thoughts as someone growing up in a Southern Baptist home inside the Bible belt; someone who was forced to attend church every Sunday until they were eighteen years old. I didn't believe in any of it. In fact, I was secretly doing spells in my room and reading zines about the occult and other esoteric topics. Zines were a medium for me to write about my discoveries.

During my junior year of high school, I started distributing one of my zines at school anonymously and in my senior year, I was ratted out and suspended. My parents were furious, especially my mom because she wanted me to graduate as a "super senior" (someone whose GPA is whatever and has never been in trouble at school). With my suspension, I no longer qualified for that 'prestigious' title. My dad didn't understand why I was being suspended for writing a zine (even if he didn't know what I was writing about). I was angry because I was unaware until that moment that a student's constitutional rights only applied as far as the entrance to the high school. Once inside, all bets were off. I wanted to fight the system. I wanted to rally and protest the patriarchy and the oppressive nature of the Indiana educational system. I wanted to burn down the establishment, but my parents forbade it. They wanted me to take my suspension, graduate, and move on with my life. So that is what I did. I spent my suspension chain smoking cigarettes and listening to my Walkman while mowing the lawn. To be fair, we had a huge yard to mow, around five acres, so it was a punishment of sorts.

Fortunately, I didn't let that suspension derail my zine creation. I simply didn't bring any of them to school. Over the years the titles, themes, and layouts of my zines have changed, evolved, and matured along with me. I have made some wonderful life-long friends through zines, and we have tabled and attended zine fests together all across the U.S. The zine world is a magickal place, and I am honored to still be a part of the community, despite being forty-nine years old now and feeling irrelevant most days. Zines are a part of my identity, my healing, and the way I position myself in teaching and learning environments. Zines give power and voice back to those our oppressive systems have purposely tried to silence. Zines give folx the chance to share their stories on their own terms. Zines moves us from cultural consumers to cultural producers of information. Zines are one of the most powerful forms of critical creativity and one of the most time intensive. Despite their cut-and-paste look, they are not easy to make. Every time I teach zines, someone in the class makes the mistake of waiting until the week the zine is due to start, despite my constant warnings that this decision is a huge mistake. Again, critical creativity is not an easy way out of learning. It is just a different path.

I am the Zine Librarian (among other things) at Salem State University.

When I started the position in summer 2019, the first thing I wanted to do was start a zine collection. I donated a few zines from my personal collection to get it started, but my hope was that the collection would be predominately created by SSU students. For that to happen, I had to find faculty who wanted to assign zines to their classes. Frequently, I am asked how I was able to incorporate zines into so many different courses in the last ten years across two very different institutions. What was the trick in getting faculty to take this risk? The answer is part luck and part persistence. No matter what type of institution I work at, I know that there are educators who are tired of assigning and reading research papers. They haven't moved away from it simply because they have not found an acceptable replacement. Zines can be that replacement. At Simmons University, I reached out to a faculty member who seemed cool. She taught a lot of courses around inequality, and I passionately believed that zines would pair nicely with her course content and objectives. It turns out that she was desperately trying to find something else to do with the class, something that would deeply resonate with the students. She was not 100% sold on the idea that zines would resonate as she believed the students were too digitally driven to embrace analog. She was delighted to be proven wrong. The students loved reading and creating zines. What started out as a semester trial turned into the final project for that class every semester. Students took the course oftentimes because of the zine component.

What was beautiful about the zines was the blending of research and personal narratives. Over time we tweaked the grading rubric and assignment based around the pitfalls we had encountered in previous semesters. The students worked in groups, selected any topic they wanted under the umbrella of inequality, and created content that blended their research and their experiences. On the last day of class, each group presented their zines. There were always tears both from the presenters and the witnesses. The zines were powerful, inspiring, and unique. What was so fascinating was that despite the same topics chosen over and over each semester, each zine was wildly different because each student was different and brought different elements and perspectives to the zine. Topics ranged from police brutality, trans rights, intimate partner violence, to body politics, beauty standards, and cultural appropriation. With the students' permission, I scanned their zines, and they became part of the digital student zine collection, housed by Simmons University Archives.

Once one professor takes the risk and sees good results others will follow simply by word of mouth. What started as one Sociology class branched out into Communications and Media, English, Social Work, and Gender and Women's Studies. Each professor approached zines a little differently, but we were a community of practice, developing shared learning goals and objectives. When I left Simmons in 2019, almost half of my instruction sessions were centered around zines. When I started at Salem State, I didn't know anyone interested in zines, so I decided to do a little fishing expedition. At Simmons, I sent emails to the departments I liaised for at the beginning of every semester to remind them of the types of instruction I offer, from in-class instruction sessions to brief introductions. I also had a paragraph about incorporating zines into their course design. When I drafted my first emails to faculty at Salem State, I decided to keep that paragraph about zines and see if anyone reached out. That paragraph piqued the interest of several faculty members. During my first semester, I incorporated zines into three courses: one in Biology, one in Interdisciplinary Studies and the other in Sociology. It was amazing! The professors I worked with were curious about zines (had never heard of them) and were *so over* research papers. Zines were the perfect solution.

The student feedback from that semester was mind blowing! Students loved creating zines and really felt that they learned the course material. They appreciated the ability to incorporate themselves into their research and the chance to humanize important topics, such as climate change, systematic oppression, conservation biology, and the prison industrial complex. Their ability to incorporate personal narratives and experiences into their research not only provided an extra layer of depth but provided the necessary ability to humanize their research and create content that mattered to a wider audience than just their professor. They knew going into the project that the zines could be digitized so that anyone could see their work. The element of an unknown audience motivated the students to put their best research forward and provide evidence of why this topic is so important, not just for society, but to themselves, their families and communities. The personal is political and they showed that repeatedly with their blending of research, personal stories and photographs, handmade drawings, sketches, painting, and data visualization.

That first semester ended with around 20 student-group zines from those three courses. Since that time, our student-created zine collection has over 200 physical zines and over 50 digitized zines. Because of the pandemic, there is a backlog of student zines to be digitized and more added to the pile every semester. As of this year, I will have worked with over 10 courses that have incorporated zines into the course curricula. I am synonymous on my campus with zines. It is an honor and a privilege to care for and curate the zines the students create. I've also been blessed with opportunities to partner with student organizations like the Intersectional Feminist Collective and the civic leaders from the civic engagement office. Anytime someone wants to know more about zines, I'm more than happy to talk, sometimes way longer than I should.

The type of zines the faculty are assigning their students usually require me being embedded in a course as its more than just introducing zines. I'm there in the zine workshop where the students brainstorm their topics and in all the sessions where students are putting their zines together. I help copy images and content for them (so they don't use up their own copy money) and photocopy their finished zines. My favorite day of the semester is the one where the students present their zines. Most faculty do a 'zine fest' where students take turns sitting with their zine and talking to their classmates about their zine. There is usually a peer review component as well as a positive feedback sheet that each student leaves with. The most surprising thing for faculty (and what they don't believe when I tell them) is how much students love to talk about their zines. In fact, even the shyest of students want their peers to know why they chose that image, font style, background color, etc. They are so invested in research that every piece of it matters. It's something we don't see when assigning research papers.

I believe the reason why students feel so empowered to talk about their zines is their ability to use their authentic voice. Academic writing is not creative writing. The research voice is not an authentic voice. Scholarly articles are without emotion and personality as they should be, but some students cannot fit inside that box. I, for one, would seriously rather go to the dentist than have to write a scholarly paper. I get it and I also understand the value in writing research papers. For students like me who need to hear their voice in their work in order to connect with it, zines are the perfect conduit. Peter Elbow (1998, p. 304) writes in his book *Writing with Power: Techniques for Mastering the Writing Process*, "one thing follows from it [hypothesis about voice] that's more important than anything else: everyone, however inexperienced or unskilled, has real voice available; everyone can write with power" (p. 304). Zines are one way for students to (re)discover their voice and use it to share their research and expertise. I have a motto I share with those students who struggle to find their voice in their work. It is *first you recover it then you reclaim it*. Students have to find their authentic voice first which means they need practice. Just like with active imagination, "most children have real voice but then lose it. 'Shhh' is the response we often get to the power of our real voice" (Elbow p. 309). I don't shush students inside the library, and I definitely don't want to shush them inside of the classroom. I want students to have every opportunity to recover and use their voice so that they can reclaim their power and use it to make change. Zines are just one method of reclaiming.

Mini-zines

The beautiful thing about zines is that there is no one way to do them. I've made zines with students where I was not embedded in the course. In these sessions, I talk about the power of zines and then we make mini-zines. These are a perfect introduction to zines and the students get to learn a new skill that can be shared with others. Mini-zines are low stakes. They are literally made with one single piece of copier paper. All that is required is one cut using scissors (or by running your fingers over the crease enough times to tear it smoothly). Students can make mini-zines about their teaching philosophy, their majors, career paths, who they are and what's important to them, summaries, and anything else that ties into the course content. Mini-zines take about 5 minutes to teach and then the rest is creative play. Magazines to cut up, scissors, glue sticks and pens are good supplies to bring but not necessary. Anyone can make a mini-zine. Anyone. My 5-year-old has made a mini-zine. I've had young kids make mini-zines about their family, their pet, and their favorite tv shows. A *how to* mini-zine is great to assign if faculty want to incorporate zines but don't know how. Everyone knows how to do something. I've seen minis range from how to boil water to how to not pet the cat.

Class Zine

Another type of zine that can be incorporated into any class is the class zine. Usually, I come into a class and talk about zines, then every student is given a handout and a zine page. The handout has a series of prompts to help guide them when creating their zine page. The questions range from *what class are you most excited to take, where did you grow up, what do you hope to do after college,* and *have you ever met anyone famous.* Each student will create their own page detailing a little about themselves. I bring stickers and gel pens for them to decorate their content. After class, I take the collected zine pages and put them together into a class zine where every student gets a copy. The cool thing about this is that students have a record of their classmates and can learn more about them in a passive way, which takes the pressure off of the most reserved students. Another cool thing these zines do is provide a glimpse into who they were. By the time the semester draws to a close, the students will have grown (mentally, emotionally, spiritually, intellectually) and it's a visual reminder how far they have come.

The other type of class zine I have helped faculty implement is more like a textbook. Students created zine pages that illustrated what they were learning in class. It is a collaborative document of shared knowledge. Each week students were required to turn in a set number of pages with the freedom to address the week's discussion prompt, scenarios based on weekly readings, or something they found interesting and wanted to expand on using what they learned in class. The one caveat was that no matter what they chose to focus their pages on, they had to create four questions to invite the reader into their work and engage in critical conversations. Students were encouraged to recommend a few resources for further research. The zine pages were so different, even when students chose the same prompt. The beauty was that each student read the same resources, sat through the same class discussions but experienced and embodied the content very differently, and reflected on meaning-making in diverse ways.

The intimacy with the course materials was evident in their completed pages and stood as evidence of a truly embodied teaching and learning practice. Each week, students shared their pages, and time was allotted for answering the critical questions they posed in their pages. These questions sparked in-depth and meaningful conversations led and informed by the students themselves. Together they grappled with often difficult and challenging material.

On the last day of class, each student received a digital copy of the textbook. They were excited to see it, to share it with their friends and family. I won't sugarcoat this. This takes a lot of planning, tweaking, and playing. It also takes a certain amount of risk in letting students have some control over course content and discussion, but what faculty get back is immeasurable. They get a classroom of engaged learners who want to contribute to the conversation and share their work with their peers. What better way to prepare students for contributing to the world's information landscape than by having them create their own course textbook. A literal map of their academic and personal journey of a semester's worth of (un)learning and discovery.

Handouts as Zines

What if no one at your institution wants to make zines? I don't think this is true but for arguments sake, let's say you are the only one who cares about zines. You can still use zines in your teaching. One easy way to share zines is by turning your instruction handouts into mini-zines. I created a mini-zine around brainstorming a topic and students love it. The mini-zine is designed for them to write in it as they answer questions pertaining to the different aspects of brainstorming. I find students are far more willing to fill out the mini-zine than they are a handout. They also take the mini-zines with them as opposed to leaving the worksheets behind. The mini-zine serves a few purposes. One, it takes a boring handout and makes it exciting. Two, its uniqueness makes students want to take it with them and three, because they take it with them, they now have my contact information. It's a win-win. I have another mini-zine I hand out for first-year students that is all about what the library can do for them. I find that when I go into first-year writing courses with a mini-zine, I at least get them thinking about the library in a new way.

Zine Collections

Not every institution that uses zines in the classroom has a zine collection, but it might be something to consider if you have enough classes making zines. When I started the zine collection at Simmons University, I had not made any faculty connections. However, I believed that if I had some zines to show faculty, it would help them conceptualize and hopefully persuade them to take a chance. There are numerous places to purchase zines online and I recommend doing a zine on Etsy. I try to always buy directly from the zinesters themselves and when that isn't possible, I buy from my favorite bookstore, Quimby's in Chicago. Regardless of how you start a zine collection, I recommend doing an environmental scan so you have a sense, not only of the topics and subjects your students are researching, but that you can find partners across the library and campus to help you make a strong proposal. Depending on the type of institution you work for, there might not be a cataloger who is thrilled to do original cataloging. In fact, if you are short staffed like most of our places of work, the cataloger might not have much time to devote to original cataloging. Here is where you might have to get creative.

There are ways around cataloging and barcoding zines. While I wish the zines at Salem State circulated, we don't have the bandwidth to catalog them. To circumvent this issue, I catalog all the zines myself using a free program called Librarika. In order for me to catalog student-created zines, the students have to fill out a submission form. This form not only grants me permission to make a hard copy of their zine but also to digitize it. The form is super important, not just for permission, but for capturing zine summaries written by the students themselves. Because I talk about subject headings and classification systems with the classes that create zines, the students know how important and problematic the Library of Congress Subject Headings are. I put the power in the students' hands to tell me what the subject headings are for their zines. Because I am not using LCSH in Librarika, we have a robust set of subject headings that match student voices and experiences.

Having this level of trust with the students and their zines is something I don't take lightly. Zines are not like other types of student writing. Their zines are often deeply personal, intimate and sometimes vulnerable. There is an ethics of care I follow when handling student-created zines. One of the most important aspects of my job as the Zine Librarian is to protect the work of the students. Since zines are not like other types of resources, there is always an option for students to have their zine removed from the catalog at any point. If a day comes when a student no longer wants their zine digitized or part of the physical zine collection, all they have to do is email us and let us know. We pull the zine. No questions asked. I honor their truths, their stories, and their willingness to share their expertise and experiences with an unknown audience. This is my sacred duty. This is reciprocity.

I'm always happy to chat with folx about starting zine collections and have recently consulted with several public libraries along the North

Shore here in Massachusetts. Communities are rich with stories, local history, and talent. Having a zine collection that speaks to and about the community is a truly unique way to collaborate with folx in the community while also bringing them into the library. For a few years I ran zine clubs for teens in my local public library and it was always so fun to watch kids get jazzed about writing and publishing their short stories, poems, comics, and whatever else lights them up. Zines are a great way to work with archives and create zines around local history as well as genealogy groups who might want to share interesting tidbits about local 'celebrities.'

The truth is everyone has a story to tell. People are endlessly fascinating and if given the chance, can provide a tapestry of experiences and knowledge. I wholeheartedly believe that zines are for everyone because anyone can make a zine. From toddlers to our most senior community members, if we take the time to connect with them and offer the space for their stories to be shared, I guarantee there will be folx who have been waiting for an opportunity to be heard and what better way to communicate with others than by starting a zine collection written by community members.

Research Smashbooking

My journey in writing this book has been accompanied by a smashbook. It serves as a container for all my ideas, artwork, and journaling throughout my writing process. I admit that this is the first time I have ever kept a smashbook for research and I am stoked to talk about its importance and impact on my writing and research journey.

Smashbooking is a combination of an artist book and writing journal. I first heard about smashbooking from my friend Sage who took a course called *Cosmic Smashbooking* with Catt Z. I was intrigued so I signed up for the next course. What I am drawn to most in the smashbooking process is how our subconscious mind informs our thoughts and intrapersonal rhetoric. Smashbooking is a way to visually see how our thoughts, emotions, feelings, and yes, research, inform and impact the way we live, view, and respond to the world around us. I have created several smashbooks over the past few years that have allowed me to work through creative blocks, tap into my subconscious mind, and engage in critical creativity. When I started compiling all my notes for this book, I decided to try keeping a research smashbook to help conceptualize and keep track of my thoughts. I was surprised to learn what an important role the research smashbook would have in my writing process. It was where I sketched out ideas and created images and worksheets. I doodled and free wrote, made collages, and sometimes just put down paint to move energy around. The smashbook is a powerful container that documented my research journey.

I mentioned earlier that I've had students keep journals in previous courses I have taught. They always end up being a mixture of writing and art, chronicling the students' journey throughout the course. I wasn't referring to this process as smashbooking, but it was the same idea. Their journals served as a container for all the in-class activities and discussions we had just as the smashbook was a container for my research process. I want to be clear that I never read the students' journals as I believe it would have hindered their ability to write truthfully and really engage in authentic self-reflection. I know there were a few students who did not do the journaling and ultimately it was disadvantageous to them. I could tell which students did the journaling by how engaged they were in class. Students were required to bring their journals to class and keep all their class notes inside it, but I never once asked to read them.

So how does one do smashbooking? The good news is that there is no right or wrong way to do it. Students can be as creative and involved as they want to be. Having art supplies at the ready is extremely helpful as again, most students won't be coming to class with scissors, glue sticks, and gel pens. For the class that I taught, each of the in-class activities was completed inside their smashbook, such as the pillars of strength, sketchnoting, and critical reflection writing. It's good to have some dedicated class time where smashbooking can take place. I always left twenty minutes or so for critical creativity but if time is an issue, students could complete the activity outside the classroom.

What makes a smashbook different from other types of journaling is the *smashing*. In order to quiet the intrapersonal rhetoric, a disruption must occur. *Smashing* pages is a physical disruption that invites students to literally crumple up the pages inside the notebook before they write a single word. There is something intimidating about a crisp blank sheet of white paper. For some students they feel overwhelmed by that emptiness while others don't want to mess up perfectly good sheets of paper with crap writing. There is a pervasive myth around the finished product that silences the process of creating (or writing and researching) that *good* writers do *good* writing effortlessly.

By disrupting this myth, we can make room for students to play, to take risks, to literally see the process of creating and all its messiness. Here's that transparency piece again. If we never give students an opportunity to see the mistakes and missteps in research, their own fears around perfection will prevent them from ever making a single mark on the page. They will fold under the weight of self-doubt, but a crumpled piece of paper is different! It's not perfect and therefore, it doesn't matter if they add something imperfect to it. There is freedom in a crumpled piece of paper. Freedom to create, the permission to be messy.

For most students, this is a step in the research process they have been waiting for: the permission to be imperfect. There are always a few students who simply cannot crumple up a whole notebook worth of paper, and when this happens, I encourage the crumpling of at least the first few pages to see how they feel. If they absolutely cannot do it, I do not force it. It just means this is not the method for them and I will work with those students to find alternatives.

I will model the process of smashbooking by sharing with you how I used one in the writing of this book. Once all the pages were crumpled, I did a few free writing sessions to get my ideas flowing. On days when I felt overwhelmed by the process of writing a book, I put down watercolor just to literally move energy around. Sometimes I made random marks with colored pencils to relax my mind, body, and spirit. Other times I ripped out images from magazines and glued them down in collage format to work through my writing struggles and self-doubt. There were pages of sketchnotes where I was working through some ideas and concepts. In the end, all the infographics, posters, and images inside this book were sketched out in my smashbook first before I recreated them in Canva. I worked and reworked my outline countless times within my smashbook, wrote notes to myself for the second draft, and kept a lineage list of books I needed to read that would be helpful in the writing process. I wrote letters to my future self when I felt like I couldn't finish this project. I reminded myself that I have something to say and that it matters. I also did all the activities I mentioned throughout this book in some form inside my smashbook as it is an extension of this book, a compendium, if you will. I'm not sure I can publish the smashbook, but it would be an interesting thing to do, as it reveals so much about my thought process and how I worked through each stage of writing this book. Maybe the smashbook can be viewable on some future website of mine.

The smashbook is the container for the research process: for brainstorming, gathering bits of information, doodling, gluing down images, or other bits of ephemera that speak to the research and get the student into the creative mindset. The smashbook is about making connections between the students, their research or learning process, and the resources at their disposal. It's about creative play, critical reflection, and a safe space to lay down thoughts, feelings, and new ideas. When students can safely put down their fears and anxieties inside a container that is for their eyes only, it is an opportunity to move through whatever they are feeling, bring it to the crumpled page, and leave it there. It's a chance to visually see a disruption in their intrapersonal rhetoric and hopefully a chance to gain more confidence in their power and their expertise.

They get to be messy. There are not a lot of spaces in academia or in research/teaching/learning where students have permission to be messy. Smashbooking is a practice of active listening and mindfulness. If students truly listened to their inner knowledge, what would they hear? If they could trust their intuition, what could they (re)discover? If we, as educators, provided the space for our students to be critically and creatively vulnerable, how might this shift impact and influence other areas of their lives outside the classroom? How might these small disruptions reunite us all with our spirituality that has been missing inside the classroom? In a world that needs more empathy? We need a revolution of consciousness otherwise "any external changes we make will be hollow and short-lived" (Brehm, 2021, xiii). I'm tired of being hollowed out. I think our students are too.

Can such a revolution of consciousness take place inside the classroom? Within an instruction session? What if we reframed these questions and asked *how can such a revolution of consciousness take place inside the classroom? How can it happen within an instruction session?* (Langer, p. 34). I am hopeful that some of the answers are inside this book.

The Work

Reflection Questions

- If you push against dominant narratives, what do you fear you will lose?

- What boxes has society put you in? Do you feel stuck inside any of them? Where would you like to be instead?
- What does a revolution of consciousness look like to you in regard to library instruction?

Reflection Activities
- Map out your pillars of support. Who or what holds you up?
- Create a smashbook. Continue to practice the exercises and techniques in this book in your smashbook.
- Make a zine about this book and any shifts or transformations that occurred.

Epilogue

Hey friend, I see you!

I have taught enough workshops, courses, and one-shots to know when and where the pushback will come. I deeply appreciate and recognize some very real and difficult roadblocks to overcome. First, our entire educational system in the United States needs an overhaul. We have moved from teaching the whole student to teaching whatever parts of them that will score high on standardized testing. This is to the detriment of all of us. As educators, we are only doing what our administration forces us to do. And the administration is doing what the state government and the federal government dictate. In this country, we do not place significant value on liberal arts, creativity, soul exploration, and spirituality. This movement away from teaching the whole person is ultimately making it harder for students to experience empathy and see themselves in the coursework they are assigned to do. Without empathy, we exist with fear, anxiety, and suspicion of each other, especially of folx who look different than us.

The cost of education in this country is out of control. So many young people graduate from university with $70,000 and more in student loan debt. For the next several decades, these graduates will be strangled with exorbitant monthly student loan payments and jobs that barely cover the rising cost of living. When the expense of college is exorbitant, there is no time to take liberal arts courses or other types of critical creativity classes that speak to students on a holistic level. Not when they need to get their degrees as soon as possible to save money. There simply is no time for creative play. So many students will never know that they love painting because they never had the opportunity to try it. So many students will never know if poetry would have helped them make sense of the world because they simply could not afford that kind of elective. This is sad and deeply troubling because we keep chipping away at their emotional and spiritual selves to the point where our students don't feel comfortable being creative anymore. They simply don't see a point in creative play or even take the extra time to see and hear another person.

I wholeheartedly think academia focuses too much on grades. Students want to see rubrics for every assignment with points assigned to each facet. They want to know what needs to be done so that they can get the grade they expect, nothing more, nothing less. This type of transactional learning leaves absolutely no room for subjectivity. Art, creativity, and spirituality are all subjective and require critical thinking to make sense of the world around them. I am a huge proponent of contract grading and wish it could be adopted in more courses. Contract grading puts the control of the students' grades in their hands. It is a collaborative process between the instructor and the student, and it diminishes students' anxieties and fears over grading. While most librarians, like me, are not able to implement contract grading it doesn't mean we cannot advocate for it. Having these critical conversations with faculty is one way we can push for more empathetic and holistic teaching and learning practices.

Faculty, instructors, teachers, and librarians are tired. Whether fighting for tenure, reappointment or job security, risk-taking is often not rewarded. Our job securities mostly rely on publishing, research, and good performance reviews. Teaching and the impact we have on our students is secondary when truthfully it should be the most important thing. I've heard so many professors over the years talk about how much they hate teaching, especially undergraduates. They would rather do their research and publish their findings. But isn't university about teaching? Isn't our job to help students (un)learn content? Shouldn't our institutions reward excellent teaching? In a utopian society, the answer would be 'yes.' Universities are run like businesses and all that matters is the bottom financial line. There is no income generation in empathy making at least not an income one can see and physically hold in their hands. So that leaves us to find whatever inroads we can to bring holistic teaching into our learning spaces. In academia this might look like first-year seminars, learning communities, or some equivalent where we can work with faculty who have a strong desire to do something different. If you work outside of academia, maybe inroads look like workshops, seminars, one-shots, or pop-ups inside the library you occupy.

I'm sure this sounds all too familiar to folx. I don't know what your financial situation is, and I assume that if you are teaching and educating you are doing so because you love it and you need the money. So, while making inroads is great and we know that students need this kind of creativity and holistic learning in classroom spaces, I am not advocating or suggesting we do this labor for free. Our expertise is important and should be compensated for. Unless we are independently wealthy or have the means to donate our time, we can't let capitalism take advantage of us any more than it already does. We all know that librarianship is not a huge money-making occupation nor is teaching in general. While the media loves to publish stories about selfless teachers purchasing all the school supplies for their classroom, the truth is, the institutions should be investing in student learning and well-being, not just the educators themselves. Businesses only care about the bottom dollar and cutting operating costs at every turn even if it means hurting their constituents in the process.

All of this is to say push back where we can. Take risks only if it is safe for us to do so. Take small steps. Let the changes start on a microcosmic level and ripple out. Find folx we can partner with. In my experience, sometimes all it takes is for one or two faculty members, community members, and/or colleagues to take a chance with you. There is safety in numbers and buy-in. Once other folx see the thing we are doing and how awesome it is for 'so and so', others will come knocking on our door. I guarantee it. I used to tell the graduate students I worked with to form their *Ocean's 11* at every place they work. I am not good at all the things, nor do I know all the things. So, I find folx that have more experience, different viewpoints, expertise, and educational backgrounds than me and we work together to find creative solutions. We need to let this work inspire others to try new things and step outside their circles. Allow ourselves to be the 'creative one' who sparks inspiration and enthusiasm among those we interact with. Someone has to lead the way for educating with empathy and it might as well be us!

Before I wrap up, I want to share with you my teaching statement. I've applied to various jobs during my professional career and some institutions require a teaching statement along with the application materials. My teaching statement has evolved over the years as I have learned more, matured, and found my specific niche (calling). Today, my teaching is supported by the educating with empathy framework. I wanted to share with you how I discuss this framework within the context of teaching and librarianship. Maybe something will resonate with you.

Teaching Statement

I practice educating with empathy which recognizes the unique lived experiences of each student in the classroom. Research and the teaching of it begin with conversation and being empathetic of where students are in the moment. When teaching, I take a holistic approach. When students come into the classroom, they bring their whole selves, past, and present which shapes the way they understand and interact with information. I strive to build a sense of community in the classroom where we not only actively listen to one another but learn from each other. I believe that students are experts of their own lived experiences. When space is made for students to share their expertise, opportunities arise that create for them deeper connections to not only information sources but the entire research process. Stories build community, but more importantly, they remind us we are not alone. When I create space for experiential learning, students begin to see themselves in the research and become invested in the research process. One way I achieve community in the classroom is by acknowledging students have knowledge and expertise. Through conversation, students share how they find information, where they search, and how they evaluate what they find. Through think/pair/share activities, students learn from and alongside each other, making space for different ways of learning and knowing. I see the classroom as a shared space where learning happens laterally as opposed to lecture or 'sage on the stage' styles of teaching.

Education is a life-long process that continues beyond the walls of academia. So much of what I teach students in terms of database searching and locating library resources will become inaccessible to them upon graduation. In contrast, the research skills and evaluation methods I share with students set them up to be successful in not only their careers but in their lives as well. In 2017 (Stahura, 2018), I created the ACT UP evaluation method after much reflection on paywalls and institutional access to resources. ACT UP is a useful acronym for critically evaluating resources while also taking privilege in publishing into consideration. I teach this method widely and I have seen the difference it has on the quality of resources students find and cite in their assignments. With this method, I've had the privilege of helping students locate information that is more inclusive and responsive to the communities they are calling in (out). I've been humbled by the various institutions that have adopted the ACT UP method into their classrooms and instructional methodologies. From universities to social justice groups, ACT UP is empowering because it centers privilege and intention.

My role as a librarian encompasses all these facets and more. As a librarian, I am often the first point of contact for students. This interaction is crucial for building trust which is why I practice empathy. I want students to feel comfortable asking for help. I believe the role of librarianship is more than just educating students to become better researchers and information seekers. My role as a librarian and educator is about creating lasting change and making spaces for students to explore and interact with a variety of sources and ideas on a more personal level. Successful instruction sessions and research consultations empower students to dig deeper, step outside their comfort circles, and produce work that best represents who they are. When I say I am a librarian, I am calling in aspects of myself such as artist, educator, and zinester, and oftentimes counselor and social worker. These aspects bring different skill sets and ways of knowing that help inform the way I approach students and their research needs. When I say I work in the field of librarianship I call out privilege in publishing and the power of semantics and call in the diverse ways of learning and knowing. For me, being a librarian is holding space between novice and expert learners so that those who walk into the space can be challenged and encouraged to learn and try something new. It's holding space for change in whatever form it needs to take.

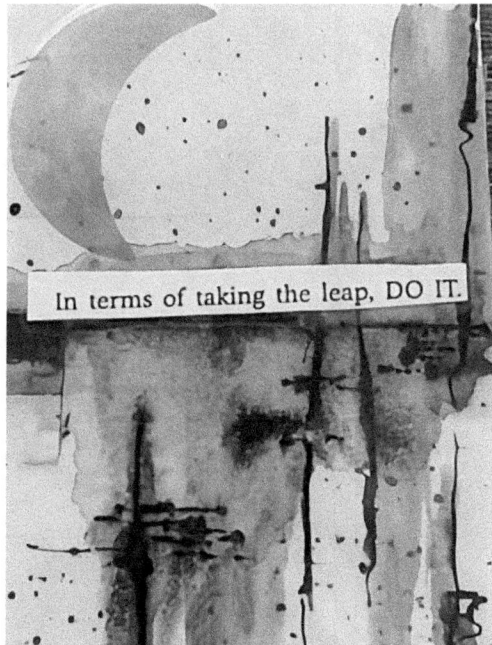

Image created by
Dawn Rogers Stahura

If you enjoyed this book and implemented some of the ideas into the way you educate, I'd love to hear about it. Just like research, change does not exist in a vacuum. We have to share with others our successes and our failures. Transparency is so important. If you use social media, you can tag your work with #educatingwithempathy. I look forward to joining creative forces with you. Whoever and wherever you are. You are not alone on this journey. I'm just up ahead, holding the light for you.

Supplementary material

I've mentioned a lot of resources throughout this book, most of which I created. I want to share these resources with you. They are available under the following Creative Commons license:

Attribution-NonCommercial-ShareAlike 4.0 International (CC BY-NC-SA 4.0)

You can access the supplemental materials at my website: www.dawn-stahura.com under *Educating with Empathy*. At the end of the day what matters most to me is that the knowledge, experiences, and resources I share in this book resonates and inspires you to educate with empathy.

Let's do this.

References

Astin, A. W. (2004). Why spirituality deserves a central place in liberal education. *Liberal Education, 90*(2), 34–41.

Barry, L. (2014). *Syllabus: Notes from an accidental professor.* Drawn & Quarterly.

Brehm, J. (2021). *The dharma of poetry: how poems can deepen your spiritual practice and open you to joy.* Simon and Schuster.

Brown, B. (2010). *The gifts of imperfection.* Hazelden.

Brown, B. (2010). *The power of vulnerability* [Video]. TED Conferences. https://www.ted.com/talks/brene_brown_the_power_of_vulnerability?utm_campaign=tedspread&utm_medium=referral&utm_source=tedcomshare

Burvall, A., & Ryder, D. (2017). *Intention: Critical creativity in the classroom.* Blend Education.

Cocoa/Puss. (n.d.). *All my best friends have herpes.* [Zine]

Concordia University's Art Hive Network. (2018). *Community listening circles.* Art Hive.

Duckworth, S. (2019). *How to sketchnote: A step-by-step manual for teachers and students.* Elevate Books Edu.

Elbow, P. (1998). *Writing with power: Techniques for mastering the writing process.* Oxford University Press.

Glazer, S. (Ed.). (1999). *The heart of learning: Spirituality in education.* Tarcher/Putnam.

Goodchild, M. (2020, September 29). *Integrating Indigenous knowledge for system change.* Collective Trauma Summit with Thomas Hbl.

Hannah. (2005). *Small magic.* [zine].

Hersey, T. (2022). *Rest is resistance: A manifesto.* Little, Brown Spark.

hooks, b. (1994). *Teaching to transgress: Education as the practice of freedom.* Routledge.

hooks, b. (2001). *All about love: New visions.* HarperCollins.

Jevons, F. B. (1908). The definition of magic. *Sociological Review* 1(2), 105–17.

Jones, L. (2005). What does spirituality in education mean? *Journal of College and Character, 6(7).*

Jordan, J. (1995). *Poetry for the people: A revolutionary blueprint.* Routledge.

Jewell, T. (2020). *This book is anti-racist: 20 lessons on how to wake up, take action, and do the work.* Frances Lincoln Children's Books.

Langer, E. (1989). *Mindfulness.* Addison-Wesley.

Lerner, J. E., & Fulambarker, A. (2018). Beyond diversity and inclusion: Creating a social justice agenda in the classroom. *Journal of Teaching in Social Work* 38(1), 43–53.

Karnatz, J.S. (2022). *Money magic: Practical wisdom and empowering rituals to heal your finances.* Chronicle Books.

Mcniff, S. (1998). *Trust the process: An artist's guide to letting go.* Shambhala.

Nash, R. J. (2002). *Spirituality, ethics, religion, and teaching: A professor's journey.* P. Lang.

Navickas, C. (2020). Grading contracts including sample contracts [presentation handout]. *Grading Contracts: What, Why & How.*

Okun, T., & Jones, K. (2000). *White supremacy culture. Dismantling racism: A workbook for social change groups.* Change Work. https://www.dismantlingracism.org/.

Palmer, P. J. (2003). Teaching with heart and soul: Reflections on spirituality in teacher education. *Journal of Teacher Education 54*(5), 376–85.

Peary, A. (2022). Mantra of intention. *New Writing 19(1)*, 3–12.

Tisdell, E. J., & Tolliver, D. E. (2003). Claiming a sacred face: The role of spirituality and cultural identity in transformative adult higher education. *Journal of Transformative Education, 1*(4), 368–92.

Wilson, S. (2009). *Research is ceremony: Indigenous research methods*. Fernwood Publishing.

Mentioned Works

Catt Z. (2019). *Cosmic smashbooking with Catt Z*. https://cosmicsmash-booking.com/.

Data Center: Research for Justice. (2015). *Introduction to research justice.* Datacenter.org.

Duckworth, S. (n.d.) *Wheel of power/privilege.* [image].

Freire, P. (2017). *Pedagogy of the oppressed*. Penguin.

Kelly [@kellymce] (2019, October 2). *I asked my students to invent their own citation styles and one group included the emojis that represented the feeling you had when you first read the thing.* Twitter. https://twitter.com/kellymce/status/1179456745929789440.

Salem State University. (2019). *Student created zine collection* https://digitalrepository.salemstate.edu/handle/20.500.13013/127.

Simmons University. (2021). *Student created zine collection.*https://simmons.access.preservica.com/uncategorized/SO_98b58e71-97dc-45f2-b9ca-e6fbc86ebd84/.

influential Works

Battista, A., Ellenwood, D., Gregory, L., Higgins, S., Lilburn, J., Harker, Y. S., & Sweet, C. (2015). Seeking social justice in the ACRL Framework. *Communications in Information Literacy, 9*(2), 6.

Center for Contemplative Science & Compassion-Based Ethics. (2019). *The SEE learning companion. Social, emotional & ethical learning.* Emory University.

Falout, J. (2014). Circular seating arrangements: Approaching the social crux in language classrooms. *Studies in Second Language Learning and Teaching, 4*(2), 275-300.

Good Feather, D. (2021). *Think Indigenous: Native American spirituality for a modern world*. Hay House, Inc.

Love, B.L. (2019). *We want to do more than survive: Abolitionist teaching and the pursuit of educational freedom*. Beacon Press.

Nash, R. (2013). *Our stories matter: Liberating the voices of marginalized students through scholarly personal narrative writing*. Peter Lang, Inc.

Piepmeier, A. and Zeisler, A. (2009). *Girl zines: Making media, doing feminism*. NYU Press.

Schwartz, R. (n.d.). *Getting students to do their assigned readings*. [handout].

Winters, A., & America, N. (2014). *Using talking circles in the classroom*. Heartland Community College.

Index

academic articles, 50
academic writing, 100
accountability, 40, 63, 80, 82
accountability buddies, 52, 67
accountability sessions, 66-8
ACT UP, 39, 40
ACT UP evaluation method, 38, 40–3, 54, 95, 114
active imagination, 101
active learning, 52
active listening, 18, 25, 61, 108
activism, 29, 38-40, 62
Adderley, Sage, 11, 105
agents of change, 63, 77
Alaniz, Dez, 11, 23, 61, 95
algorithmic biases, 90
Alt-Right, 76
American Library Association (ALA), 32, 39
AND movements, 70-1, 87, 91
annotated bibliographies, 95
anxiety disorder, 2
archives, 105
art for art's sake, 85-6
art-making activity, 60
art supplies, 1, 3, 55, 60, 94, 106
art therapy, 65
authentic voice, 24, 100, 101
authority, 27-8, 31, 37, 47

barcoding, 104
Barry, Lynda, 58
beginner's mind[set], 55-6
Bible, 7
Bible belt, 97
Black women, 32
Blackboard, 93
brainstorming sessions, 93
breakout rooms, 53-4
Brown, Brene, 24

Canva, 107
Canvas, 93
capitalism, 3, 31, 66-7, 76, 79-80, 86, 113
cataloging, 104
Catt Z, 105
Chad, 17, 45, 56-7
CINAHL, 82
citation circles, 62
citation style, 41, 43
Civic Engagement Office, 100
class space, 47
class zine, 102, *see also* zines

classification systems, 28, 54, 89, 104
collaborative document, 102
collage format, 107
Collins, Stacy, 59
colonialism, 85
comfort circles, 34, 48, 53, 56, 86-7, 115
communism, 76
community colleges, 15, 76
community of practice, 49, 67, 99
Concordia University's Art Hives Network, 60
Confederate flag, 7
corporations, 63
CRAAP evaluation method, 37
creative freedom, 34
creative play, 41, 52, 85, 90, 101, 108, 111-2
creative space[s], 86, 89
creative spirit, 87
critical information literacy, 28, 32, 39
critical learning/unlearning, 16, 73
critical reflection writing, 106
critical thinking skills, 76
cultural hegemony, 85

dabbling, 76
database[s], 16, 34, 40, 46, 63, 82-3, 88
DataCenter, 74
dead names, 54
deep learning, 18-9, 58, 77, 85
democracy, 37, 40
detachment, 29, 46
discussion norms, 53
disease, 75-6
disinformation, 37, 40
dominant narratives, 25, 38, 86-7, 90, 108
doodling, 60, 108
drawing[s], *see also* portrait[s], 48, 58, 65-6, 68, 82, 88-9, 90-1, 100
drawing occupations, 58
Duckworth, Sylvia, 61

eating disorder[s], 30
education system[s], 16, 25, 32, 46
Elbow, Peter, 101
email signature[s], 78, 80, 84
emotion prompts, 49
emotional side of research, 51
empathy statement, 78-9, 84
environmental scan, 104
ethics of care, 104
Etsy, 103
evaluation methods, 31, 43, 114

evaluation of information, 40
experiential knowledge, 31-3, 74-5, 78

fake news, 27, 37-8, 54
feminism, 11, 41
flipped classroom model, 60
four faces, 85
freedom of expression, 90
freedom of speech, 15

Glazer, Steven, 73
Goodchild, Melanie, 72, 75
Google (Scholar), 49, 82
grades, 2, 46, 75, 112

Haiti, 30
handouts, 40, 103
Harjo, Joy, 55
healing, 75-8, 97
Hersey, Tricia, 24
hierarchy, 47, 54
hooks, bell, 16, 24, 71

imposter syndrome, 3, 45
Indiana, 2-4, 6, 8, 32, 96-7
infographic annotated bibliographies (infographic annabibs), 95-6
information literacy, 10, 28, 32, 35, 91, *see also* critical information literacy
information spectrums, 24, 27-9, 32, 34, 57, 88
inner critic, 17, 45, 55-6, 68, *see also* Chad
inner monologue, 45
instruction session, 39, 48, 60, 77, 82, 93, 108, *see also* one-shot instruction session,
intellectual freedom, 15
intention, 18, 27, 38, 46, 54-5, 57, 88, *see also* mantra of intention
intentional play, 85
intentionality, 18, 54
intersecting identities, 14, 59, 86
Intersectional Feminist Collective, 100
intersectionality, 41, 59, 60, 70
intrapersonal rhetoric, 45, 94, 105-6, 108

Johnson, Shari, 59
Jordan, June, 19
journaling, 105-6

Kimmerer, Robin Wall, 73
knowledge systems, 29, 60

Latin, Rebecca, 59
law of attraction, 69
law of contagion, 69-71
learning process, 72, 81, 86-7, 91, 108
liberal arts education, 76
Libguide, 40
librarian(s), 14, 37-8, 40-1, 81, 96, 112-3
librarianship, 15, 17, 38, 41, 113, 115
Librarika, 104
Library Juice Academy, 32
library neutrality, 38
Library of Congress Subject Headings (LCSH), 104

library resources, 16, 41, 52, 114
lineage, 10, 20-1, 107
local history, 105

mainstream media, 50
makerspace, 68
mantra cards, 94
mantra of intention, 55, 57, 68
Massachusetts, 9, 105
McElroy, Kelly, 41
McNiff, Shaun, 65-6, 82
medium, 5, 18, 65
memes, 93
methodology section, 31, 39
mindfulness, 45-6, 57, 68, 80, 83-4, 90, 108
mindlessness, 46, 57
misinformation, 33, 37, 61
Moodle, 93
music, 8, 29, 56, 76, 84-5, 89

naming ceremony, 68
naming stories, 53-5
Nash, Robert, 71
negative thought patterns, 94
negativity, 69
Nin, Anais, 1
non-dominant hand, 92-3
non-dominant handwriting, 91, 93

one-shot instruction session, 46-7, 60

pandemic, 16, 27, 49, 100
parallel stories, 29-31
Parks, Rosa, 39
pass the popcorn, 53
patriarchal systems, 70
patriarchy, 97
Peary, Alexandria, 10, 45-6, 57
Pelonia, Nikki, 53
perfectionism, 30
permission, 17, 86, 107-8
personal narrative writing, 5, 32, 57, 88
Pike, Christopher, 8
pillars of strength/support, 91-2, 106, 109
Plath, Sylvia, 2
pop culture, 32
portrait(s), 48, 52, 89, 90-1 *see also* drawing(s)
positionality statements, 19, 61-2, 66
positive feedback sheet, 100
Presidio Research Center of Santa Barbara, 61
privilege in publishing, 41, 50, 114-5
pronouns, 48, 53
propaganda, 37
proximity to power, 48, 75
Purdue University, 3

Quimby's Bookstore, 104

race, 19, 32, 41
racism, 7, 59, 31
racist evaluation methods, 31
reciprocity, 48, 63, 104
red states, 41
relationality, 6

representation, 89
research conversation[s], 33, 49, 52, 82
research fatigue, 51
research guide[s], 40, 52 see also Libguide
research paper[s], 30-1, 46, 57, 81, 88, 93, 95, 98-100
research sessions, 66
research voice, 100
researching in community, 49
Retraction Watch website, 63
revolution of consciousness, 108-9
rubrics, 46, 83, 112
rule of three, 50

sacred spaces, 73
safe space, 108
Sage Publishing, 63
Salem State University, 98
scarcity mindset, 28, 45-7, 50-1, 67, 92, 95
scientific method, 73
searching habits, 50
self-actualization, 24
self-doubt, 107
self-expression, 86
self-talk, 46
semantics, 28, 38, 54, 60, 89, 90, 115
separation of church and state, 13, 71
sexism, 7
Sexton, Anne, 2
silos, 47
Simmons University, 57, 88, 98-9, 103
sketchnoting, 106
smashbook[s], 93, 105-9
smashbooking, 105-9
Smith-McQueenie, Lisa, 59
social justice movements, 15, 39, 59
Social Justice Training Institute, 59
social media, 37-8, 67, 116
socialism, 76
solidarity, 30, 64
Southern Baptist faith, 7, 18, 97
Southern Poverty Law Center, 59
Stahura, Rowan, 11, 55
stereotypes, 59, 61, 68, 89
storytelling, 6, 13, 54, 88
student alternative loans, 3

student engagement, 33, 47-8, 83
student-group zines, 100
student-led discussions, 58, 90-1
subconscious mind, 105
subject headings, 28, 104

template[s], 60-1, 66
tenure track, 19, 77, 112
toxic masculinity, 3
trade schools, 76
transactional learning, 78, 112
transformation(s), 18-9, 23, 25, 33, 48, 85, 87, 92, 109
transformative learning, 78, 112
transparency, 16-7, 33, 46, 51, 56, 107, 116
trust, 16, 104, 115

veiled learning, 88, 92
virtual space, 49, 53, 67
vision statements, 66
vocational awe, 41

Washington, Jamie, 59
Western ideals and knowledge systems, 29
white flight, 8
white privilege, 23, 77
white supremacy, 32-3, 44, 61, 70, 86
whiteness, 8, 32-3, 54
whitewashing, 38
Wilson, Shawn, 6
witnessing, 6, 7, 18, 23-4, 49, 63
worksheet, 59-61, 68
writing session[s], 66, 107

xenophobia, 7

zine collection at Simmons University, 103
zine fest[s], 97, 100
Zine Librarian, 98, 104
zine workshop, 100
zinesters, 11, 104
Zoom, 53, 67

www.ingramcontent.com/pod-product-compliance
Lightning Source LLC
Chambersburg PA
CBHW052052220426
43663CB00012B/2543